1954

THE NEWS THE EVENTS AND THE LIVES OF 1954

Second Edition

Pauline Watson & Elizabeth Absalom
D'Azur Publishing

Published by D'Azur Publishing 2024
D'Azur Publishing is a Division of D'Azur Limited

Copyright © D'Azur Publishing 2024

Pauline Watson and Elizabeth Absalom have asserted her rights under the Copyright, Design and Patents Act 1988 to be identified as the author of this work.

The language, phrases and terminology within this book are as written at the time of the news reports during the year covered and convey the sentiments at that time. The news reports are taken from internationally recognised major newspapers and other sources of the year in question.
The language does not represent any personal view of the author or publisher.

All Rights Reserved. No part of this publication may be reproduced, stored or transmitted in any form or by any means, electronic, mechanical, digital or otherwise, except under the terms of the Copyright, Designs and Patents Act 1988 or under terms of a licence issued by the publisher. This book is sold subject to the condition that it shall not, by way of trade or otherwise, be lent, resold or hired out, or otherwise circulated without the publishers prior consent in any form or binding or cover other than that in which it is published and without a similar condition, including this condition, being imposed on the subsequent purchaser.
All requests to the Publisher for permission should be addressed to info@d-azur.com.

First published in Great Britain in 2023 by D'Azur Publishing
Second Edition published 2024
Contact: info@d-azur.com Visit www.d-azur.com
ISBN 9798324724474

ACKNOWLEDGEMENTS

The publisher wishes to acknowledge the following people and sources:

British Newspaper Archive; The Times Archive; Cover Malcolm Watson; p8 Malcolm Watson; p12 Roland Godefroy; p12 musicfestivalexplorer.com; p12 relleborgsallehanda.se; p13 RCA Records; p16 Mercury Newspaper; p17 Jonathan Bowen - Own work; p17 Mx. Granger; p19 Graham Sutherland; p19 IMDb; p20 Diamond Mansion; p25 Phillip Law; p27 Victorian Web; p35 Simon Johnston/Sandhurst Royal Military Academy; p37 RIBA Collections; p41 John M; p41 Stevenage Museum; p43 liverpoolships.org; p47 www.cadgwith.com; p51 National Army Museum; p51 Simon Johnston/Sandhurst Royal Military Academy; p53 Σπάρτακος; p53 London Coins; p57 dalbera from Paris; p57 Roberto Fortuna; p57 Meadows Museum; p59 Environment Agency; p63 Look Up London; p65 Bullion By Post; p65 parastatidisenexyra; p67 Dave Farrance; p73 Thamesmatch.co.uk; p77 British Newspaper Archive; p79 Roseberys; p81 Malcolm Watson; p83 Walter Stoneman; p85 Abe Books; p87 Malcolm Watson; p87 Bonnie Cehovet; p89 Barts Heritage; p89 open Sandwich; p89 Calendar Customs; p93 Photo by Paul Berry on Unsplash; p93 Visit Cumbria; p95 Eszter Miller from Pixabay; p97 Eric Polk; p107 Paul J; Andy B; Philly Bell; p111 British Matchbox Label and Bookmatch Society; p113 Adib Farid; p123 lions auctioneers;

Whilst we have made every effort to contact copyright holders, should we have made any omission, please contact us so that we can make the appropriate acknowledgement.

CONTENTS

1954 Highlights Of The Year   4-5

1954 The Year You Were Born   6-7

1959 The Year You Were Five   8-9

1965 The Year You Were Eleven   10-11

1970 The Year You Were Sixteen   12-13

1975 The Year You Were Twenty One   14-15

1954 The Major Sporting Events   16-17

1954 The Major Cultural Events   18-19

1954 Science and Nature   20-21

1954 The Lifestyles of Everyday People   22-23

THE YEAR DAY-BY-DAY   **24-127**

The 1954 calendar   128

LIFE IN 1954

Monarch: Queen Elizabeth II   Prime Minister: Sir Winston Churchill – Conservative

In 1954, Winston Churchill was presiding over a period of rapid growth and increasing prosperity after the sombre years of the war. Towns and cities were reshaped by a massive building programme of council estates, tower blocks and shopping centres. Rationing ended in July, and foods not seen in the shops since the beginning of the war started to appear on shelves again.

For the first time since the war, petrol was off ration and a huge influx of cars took to the roads. Television sets mushroomed, taking up their now familiar place as the focal point of the 'sitting room' and the strange looking H-shaped aerials were clamped firmly to the chimney stacks.

It was the year of nuclear testing in the Pacific and the first nuclear submarine was launched. There was anti-Communist paranoia in America, and TV dinners became popular. The first comprehensive school in Britain opened, the first British TV soap was aired, and there was a solar eclipse.

A Nuclear Test

FAMOUS PEOPLE WHO WERE BORN IN 1954

8th March: David Wilkie, Olympic swimmer
13th March: Valerie, Baroness Amos, Politician
19th April: Trevor Francis, Footballer
26th August: Steve Wright, DJ
19th September: Mark Drakeford, Politician
24th September: Helen Lederer, Comedienne
8th November: Kazuo Ishiguro, Writer
25th December: Annie Lennox, Singer
31st December: Alex Salmond, Politician

FAMOUS PEOPLE WHO DIED IN 1954

11th January: Oscar Straus, Composer
20th January: Fred Root, Cricketer
24th March: Thanh Thai, Emperor of Vietnam
7th June: Alan Turing, Mathematician
13th July: Frida Kahlo, Artist
3rd August: Sidonie Gabrielle 'Colette', Novelist
3rd November: Henri Matisse, Artist
15 November: Lionel Barrymore, American actor
20th December: James Hilton, Novelist

News Of The Year

JANUARY USS Nautilus, the world's first nuclear submarine is launched in Groton, Connecticut, by the 1st Lady of the United States, Mamie Eisenhower.

FEBRUARY The first mass vaccination programme for children against polio begins in Pittsburgh, Pennsylvania.

MARCH The UK Atomic Energy Authority was founded. Based in Oxfordshire, it focused on fusion energy research programmes, with a view to developing fusion power as a commercially viable energy source.

APRIL Symphony conductor Arturo Toscanini suffers a temporary memory loss during a live concert broadcast in New York, and retires from public performances.

MAY Medical student Roger Bannister becomes the first person to run a mile in under 4 minutes at the Iffley Road Track in Oxfordshire.

JUNE The first solar eclipse for 38 years is witnessed by millions of people on 3 continents. Asia, America and Europe.

JULY Wartime rationing in Britain comes finally to an end after 14 years, with meat and meat products being the last to be de-restricted.

AUGUST Hand built at the Samlesbury Aerodrome in Lancashire, the English Electric supersonic fighter plane makes its maiden flight.

SEPTEMBER Kidbrooke Comprehensive School for Girls in The Royal Borough of Greenwich, London becomes the first purpose built comprehensive school in Britain.

OCTOBER The Communist Viet Minh under Ho Chi Minh occupy the country of North Vietnam, in an attempt to unify the Democratic Republic of Vietnam.

NOVEMBER In Alabama an 8lb piece of Hodge's meteorite crashes through a house roof. This is the first recorded event of a person being injured by an object from outer space.

DECEMBER The first Burger King, whose concept was inspired by the success of the McDonald's franchise, opened in Miami by Keith J. Kramer and Matthew Burns, serving basic hamburgers and milkshakes.

Films and Arts

The 26th Academy Awards were held, with **From Here To Eternity** winning eight Oscars in total. It is a romantic war drama set in Hawaii in the run up to the attack on Pearl Harbour starring Burt Lancaster, Deborah Kerr and Frank Sinatra who won a personal Oscar. Two iconic Japanese films of note were released this year: **Seven Samurai** and **Godzilla**, whilst American releases were **On The Waterfront**, starring Marlon Brando and Rod Steiger and the musical **White Christmas** starring Bing Crosby and Danny Kaye. In Britain the Ealing Studios comedy, **Belles of St. Trinians**, starring Alastair Sim, Joyce Grenfell and Sid James was very popular.

The first soap opera on television entitled **The Grove Family** was a live BBC show, portraying the daily life of a lower middle class family living in Britain after the war. On the radio, the comedy series **Hancock's Half Hour** was broadcast, starring Tony Hancock, Sid James and Kenneth Wiliams.

In the theatre the musical **Salad Days** ran first in Bristol, then moved to the West End.

J.R.R.Tolkien's fantasy novel **The Fellowship of The Ring** was published in October, closely followed by the sequel **The Two Towers** at the end of the year. William Golding's dystopian novel **Lord of The Flies** was published in September.

1954 THE YEAR

In 1954 unemployment was low, and living standards were rising rapidly. Many women who had worked during the war continued to do so, refusing to go back to 'just being a housewife'. Inevitably this led to more children being cared for out of school hours by grandparents or becoming 'latch-key kids'. The old utilitarian and heavy styles of both fashion and furnishings became a thing of the past and there was greater interest in design as fabrics were more brightly coloured with bold patterns.

A full skirt was fashionable for women, made even more exaggerated by wearing a paper nylon petticoat under the skirt, often stiffened by being dipped into a sugar solution before drying. Some young men adopted the Teddy Boy style fashion for drape coats with a velvet collar, drainpipe trousers, and suede shoes known as Brothel-creepers. Their hair was Brylcreemed and elaborately styled into a roll at the front and Duck's Arse at the back.

Britain was almost obsessed with all things American after the war and the first Wimpy Bars opened in Britain in 1954, selling hamburgers, expresso coffee and milkshakes. Named after a fat friend of 'Popeye', the Wimpy bar added the 'British' elements of waitress service and cutlery. They became very popular, especially with the decade's 'new' teenagers who welcomed the addition to the high street's coffee bars and juke boxes.

How Much Did It Cost?

The Average Pay:	£500 (£9 9s p.w)
The Average House:	£1860
Loaf of White Bread:	7½d (3p)
Pint of Milk:	7d (3p)
Pint of Beer:	1s 6d (7p)
12mnths Road Tax	£12 10s (£12.50)
Gallon of Petrol:	4s 6d (5p/litre)
Newspapers:	5d - 1s (2p)
To post a letter in UK:	2½d (1p)
TV Licence	£3 Black & White + £1 radio

Born in 1954, you were one of 51 million people living in Britain and your life expectancy then was 69.7 years. You were one of the 15.4 births per 1,000 population, but you had a 3% chance of dying as an infant from infectious diseases such as measles, mumps or rubella. However, vaccinations for polio, diphtheria, tetanus, and whooping cough became more readily available as the year progressed. Britain's cultural and social landscape was changing rapidly with more disposable income to many households. The country embarked on a massive rebuilding programme and whole new towns emerged from the rubble of the war years.

YOU WERE BORN

POPULAR CULTURE

The best-selling record of the year was **Secret Love** sung by the actress Doris Day in the film **Calamity Jane**. Other hits included **Blowing Wild** by Frankie Lane; the trumpet of Eddie Calvert with **Oh Mein Papa** and a surprise hit for the comedian Norman Wisdom with **Don't Laugh at Me 'Cos I'm a Fool**.

In January the tall, handsome baseball hero, captured the heart of the beautiful, glamorous Hollywood star and Marilyn Monroe and Joe DiMaggio were married.

JRR Tolkien published the first of his **Lord of the Rings** trilogy, **The Fellowship of the Ring**, and William Golding, his morality tale, **Lord of the Flies.**

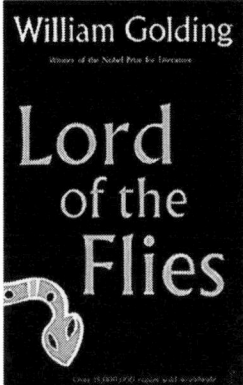

From Here to Eternity won the cinema accolades but there were other successful films this year including, **White Christmas** with Bing Crosby, **The Caine Mutiny** starring Humphrey Bogart and Kirk Douglas in **20,000 Leagues Under the Sea**.

The art exhibitions at the **Venice Biennale** are revived, introducing American abstract expressionism to Europe.

Two months after the author's death, Richard Burton made famous his 'First Voice' in Dylan Thomas's radio play, **Under Milk Wood.**

The buxom young women, fat old ladies, drunken men, honeymoon couples and vicars of Donald McGill, the artist of the 'saucy seaside postcard', led him to a £50 for breaching the Obscene Publications Act.

George Cowling gave BBC's first televised live and 'in vision' weather forecast He stood in front of the weather map, using a pencil and rubber to show the weather for the next day and informed the viewers that *tomorrow would be rather windy, a good day to hang out the washing'.*

1959 The Year

In 1959 Harold Macmillan wins the general election to give the Conservatives their record third successive term in office. The party's election slogan was, 'Life's better with the Conservatives, Don't let Labour ruin it. It was a decade of rapid economic growth and towns and cities were being reshaped by a massive building programme of council estates, tower blocks and shopping centres.

Five In 1959

Five in 1959. The UN made a declaration on the legal rights of the child to appropriate safeguarding and protection. In Britain full time attendance at school was compulsory for all 5-year-olds. Playtime was considered important at school and popular playground activities were marbles, skipping ropes, and games of Jacks or Fives. At home wooden jigsaws were popular as were cowboy sets for the boys, while girls played with dolls or helped Mother with household chores

How Much Did It Cost?

The Average Pay	£686	(£13 p.w.)
The Average House	£2,124	
Loaf of White Bread	11d	(81p)
Pint of Milk	8d	(59p)
Pint of Beer	1s 10d	(1.60)
12 Mth Road Tax	£12.10s	
Gallon of Petrol	4s 8d	(23p)
Newspapers	2½d	(0.1p)
To Post a Letter in UK	3d	(0.1p)
TV Licence B/W	£4	

The revolutionary Mini was launched in August 1959. It was driven by stars of music and fashion as well as by families on a budget. Despite the promise of the adverts, early models were slow and unreliable.

Adverts promoted it as a luxury family car but in reality, it was uncomfortable and cramped.

You Were Five

Popular Music

Pianist Russ Conway had the most top 10 entries in 1959 with six, **Side Saddle** and **Roulette** both reaching No1. Elvis Presley, Bobby Darin and Cliff Richard also peaked at No1 more than once. **Living Doll** by Cliff Richard and The Drifters is attributed to being the biggest selling single of the year. The 1958 Christmas No1, **It's Only Make Believe** by Conway Twitty stayed at No1 for four weeks in January.

JANUARY The Day the Rains Came was the first new No1 of the year for Jane Morgan.

MARCH Buddy Holly's, **It Doesn't Matter Any More** got to No1 a month after the singer had been killed in a plane crash on 3rd February. It was a two-sided hit backed with **Raining in My Heart**.

JUNE American Bobby Darin stayed at the top of the charts for four weeks with **Dream Lover** and he was No1 again in October with **Mack the Knife**.

JULY Lonnie Donegan 'The King of Skiffle' was going strong and had a No2 with **Battle of New Orleans**, more serious than his novelty hit song **Does Your Chewing Gum Lose its Flavour**.

NOVEMBER The Drifters changed their name to The Shadows and **Travellin' Light**, with Cliff Richard, was the first hit song with their new identity.

DECEMBER Teen idol Adam Faith has his first No1, **What Do You Want**. It was the shortest song to reach No1!

Health

Doctors and scientists were beginning to gather evidence that smoking could be harmful to your health, but in 1959 it was still promoted as a 'healthy', 'social' and 'fun' activity.

1965 The Year

In 1965 Britain Harold Wilson was presiding over a country where the first 'baby boomers' were due to come of age and were intent on personal freedom and permissiveness.

It was the year Sir Winston Churchill dies; Sir Stanley Matthews plays his last first division game; cigarette adverts are banned from British television; Goldie the golden eagle has 13 days of freedom from London Zoo; Ian Smith declares UDI in Rhodesia; the Certificate of Secondary Education (CSE) is first examined a s school leaving qualification; the Kray twins are arrested on suspicion of running a protection racket and Pizza Express and Kentucky Fried Chicken open in Britain.

The first English National Trail, the Pennine Way, gives walkers access to some of the country's wildest landscapes. It runs from the Peak District hills in Derbyshire, through the Yorkshire Dales and the Swaledale Valley, across the North Pennines and over Hadrian's Wall in Northumberland to the Cheviot Hills and ends in the Scottish Borders. The Trail has a *combined* ascent that exceeds the height of Mount Everest.

The End Of An Era

Sir Winston Churchill, who was Prime Minister during WW2 died in January at the age of 90. Thousands of people attended his state funeral, and it was also broadcast live on the BBC and seen around the world. During the three days of lying-in-state, 321,000 people filed past the catafalque in Westminster Hall. The funeral in Paul's Cathedral was attended by the Queen, Prime Minister, and representatives of 112 countries.

How Much Did It Cost?

The Average Pay	£1,000
The Average House	£3,350
Loaf of White Bread	1s 2½d (7p)
Pint of Milk	9½d (4p)
Pint of Beer	2s 4d (12p)
Gallon of Petrol	5s 2d (6p/litre)
Newspapers	3d – 9d (1-4p)
To Post a letter in UK	3d - 4d from May (2p)
12 Months' Road Tax	£17 10s (£17.50)
TV Licence B/W	£5 + £1 5s Radio

You Were Eleven

Popular Music & Radio

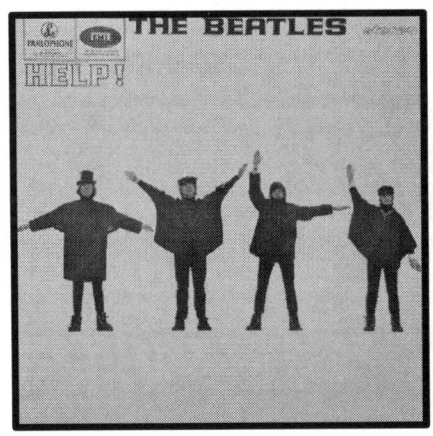

The Beatles continued to dominate the charts, with four 'Top of the Pops' during the year: **I Feel Fine** (released 1964), **Ticket to Ride**, **Help!** and **Day Tripper/We Can Work it Out**. The Seekers had three Top Ten entries in their breakthrough year, **I'll Never Find Another You** (No1) and **The Carnival is Over** (No1), but **Tears** by Ken Dodd is attributed as the biggest-selling single of the year.

JANUARY The first new number-one single of the year was **Yeh, Yeh** by Georgie Fame and the Blue Flames.

FEBRUARY Both Cilla Black and the Righteous Brothers had a hit with **You've Lost That Lovin' Feelin'** but only the Americans took it to No1.

MARCH The unknown Tom Jones took **It's Not Unusual** to the No1 slot after singer Sandie Shaw heard it as a demo and thought he was too good to give it up!

MAY Where Are You Now (My Love) was written by Tony Hatch and Jackie Trent and gave her her only No1 hit. It was featured in the TV series It's Dark Outside.

SEPTEMBER Husband and wife duo, Sonny (Bono) and Cher made their debut with **I Got You Babe** which reached No1.

NOVEMBER Get Off of My Cloud was another successful No1 for The Rolling Stones after **(I Can't Get No Satisfaction)**.

Round the Horne made its debut on BBC Radio. Kenneth Horne, Kenneth Williams, Hugh Paddick, Betty Marsden and Bill Pertwee introduced the nation to the larger than life, 'Julian and Sandy', 'J. Peasmold Gruntfuttock' and 'Rambling Syd Rumpo', all with abounding 'double entendres'.

1970 The Year

In 1970 you were old enough to get married with parental consent, and could join the army but you were too young to buy or drink alcohol in a pub, or to cast your vote in an election. In this year the Apollo 13 mission failed, but miraculously the spacecraft returned to earth and all the crew survived.

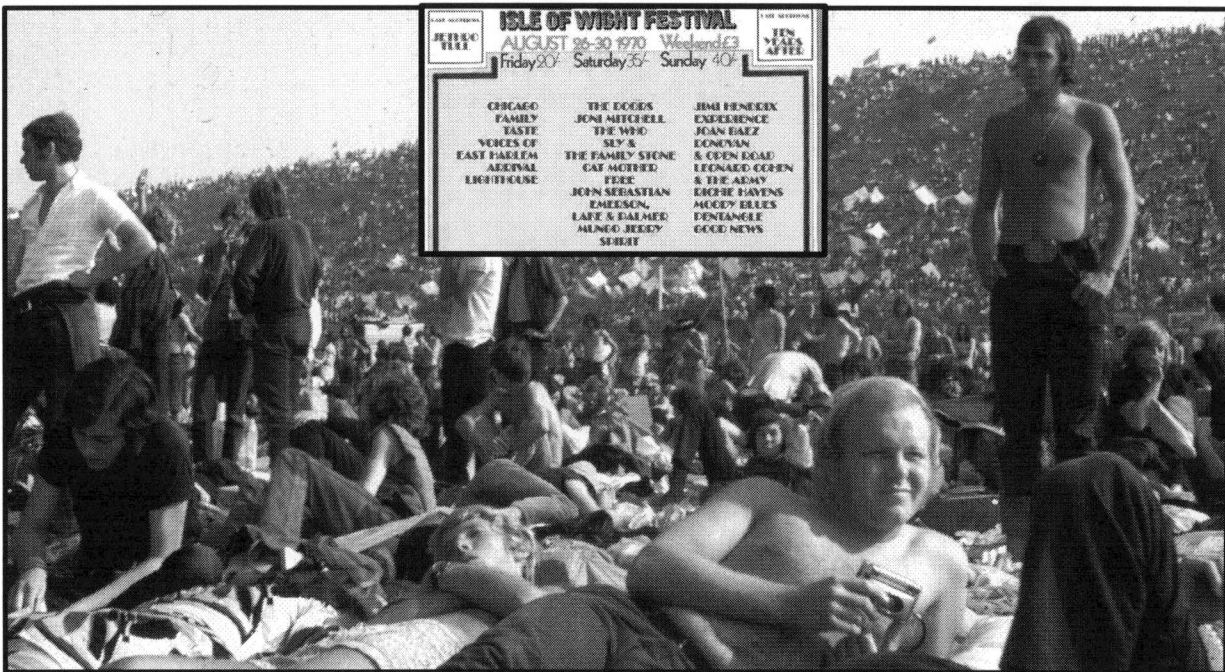

The US invaded Cambodia, and thousands of Americans protested in Washington. The Beatles shocked the music world by announcing they were disbanding, and the music festival on the Isle of Wight drew a record 600,000 crowd.

In 1970, Jimi Hendrix was rushed to a London hospital in September where he died of an overdose of barbiturates and alcohol. Sadly drug and alcohol abuse was rife among music artists at this time, and only a month later the singer Janis Joplin died of a heroin overdose.

Life at Sixteen

Sixteen in 1970, you could get a Saturday job working in a shop or supermarket which would provide you with some extra spending money, although many teenagers were expected to hand some of their wages over to their parents, to 'pay for their keep'.

You could spend your money on records, make up, or going to the cinema where the programme was always the main film, together with a supporting 'B' film. You could meet up with friends at a coffee or a Wimpy bar.

How Much Did It Cost?

The Average Pay	£1664 pa (£32pw)
The Average House	£4057
Loaf of White Bread	1s 6d (7p)
Pint of Milk	1s (5p)
Pint of Beer	2s 11d (14p)
Gallon of Petrol	6s (7p/litre)
Newspapers	5d (2p)
To Post a Letter in UK	5d (2p)
12 Mths Road Tax	£25
TV Licence	B/W £6 Colour £12

You Were Sixteen

Popular Music

Elvis Presley and The Jackson 5 shared the record for most top 10 hits in 1970 with four hit singles each. Elvis's cover of **The Wonder of You**, which topped the charts for six weeks, eventually became the second bestselling single of the year. Christie had two top-ten entries, including the number-one single **Yellow River** and Sasha Distel peaked at No 10 with **Raindrops Keep Falling on My Head** from the film, 'The Sundance Kid'

JANUARY Edison Lighthouse made their debut record with **Love Grows (Where My Rosemary Goes)** which stayed at No1 for 7 weeks.

FEBRUARY I Was Born Under a Wandering Star sung by actor Lee Marvin, was a song from the musical film Paint Your Wagon. The movie wasn't a huge success, but the record certainly was, staying at the top for 9 weeks.

MARCH Bridge Over Troubled Waters became known as Simon & Garfunkels' signature song. It was released from the album of the same name and went on to win 5 Grammie Awards.

APRIL The England Football Squad were still World Champions from 1966 when they released **Back Home** and started the tradition for celebrating the team's involvement in the international arena through songs. It topped the charts for 8 weeks.

JUNE The Bestselling single in 1970 was Mungo Jerry's **In The Summertime**, their debut single, which spent 11 weeks in the No1 spot. They couldn't find a recording of a motorcycle, so a friend who had an old Triumph sports car drove it past the studio door while one of the band held a microphone.

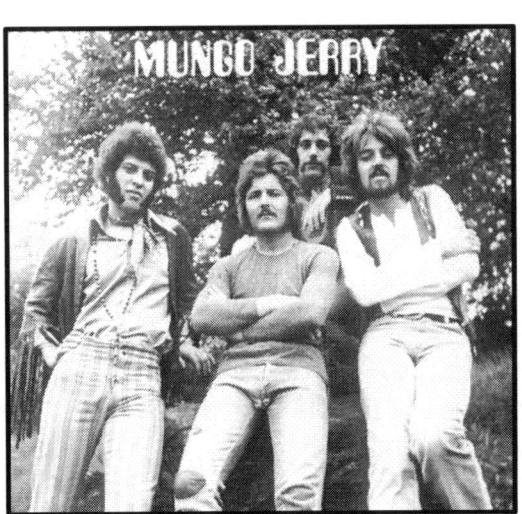

1975 The Year

1975 was a year of many contrasts and new beginnings. Unemployment rose steadily to 1.25 million by August, but the Sex Discrimination and Equal Pay Acts paved the way for a fairer society. Bill Gates founded Microsoft at the tender age of 19, and Margaret Thatcher became the first woman Prime Minister in Britain. The weather was equally astonishing with snow showers as far as London in June. The Sex Pistols made their debut in November establishing Punk Rock on the music scene, while on the TV we watched Fawlty Towers.

Package tours to sunny, warm and cheap holiday destinations were very popular. Companies such as Thompson, Horizon, Global and Clarksons all used chartered planes to fly families to booming resorts Once there, holiday makers found that in addition to the sun and sand, food and drink was much cheaper than in the UK and this led to the rapid decline in UK seaside resorts and boom in once sleepy fishing villages such as Benidorm.

On 3rd November the Forties Field was inaugurated by Her Majesty Queen Elizabeth at Aberdeen. It is the largest oilfield to be discovered so far in the British sector of the North Sea. Initially the production rate was 10,000 barrels per day, with a prospective increase to 400,000 barrels per day in the future, fuelling hopes of a steady return to better times for the country's economy.

New Route Up Everest

In September Dougal Haston and Doug Scott became the first British climbers to reach the summit of Mount Everest using the rock-climbing technique of putting fixed ropes up the South-West face of the mountain.

Doug Scott made the highest recorded bivouac at the South Summit. The expedition has been described as 'the apotheosis of the big, military-style expeditions'.

How Much Did It Cost?

The Average Pay:	£3.380 (£65 p.w)
The Average House:	£9,500
Loaf of White Bread:	15p
Pint of Milk:	7p
Pint of Beer:	18p
Gallon of Petrol:	73p (15p/litre)
12mnths Road Tax	£40
Newspapers:	5p
To post a letter in UK:	7p
TV Licence	£8 Black & White £18 Colour

YOU WERE 21

POPULAR MUSIC

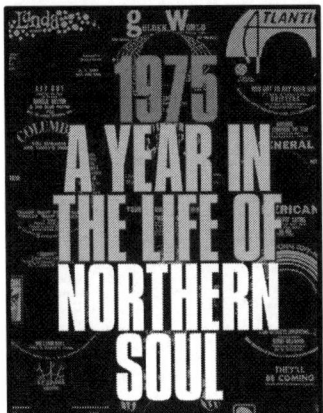 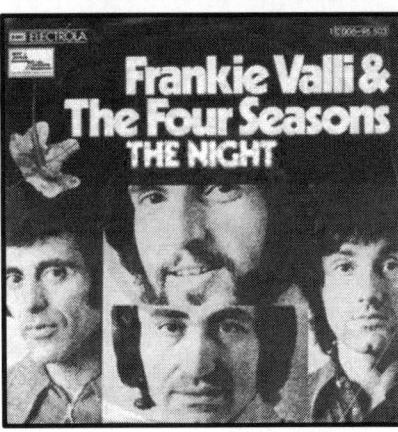 

1975 saw the burgeoning of Northern Soul in the industrial towns of England. Focusing on the rare 'B' side records of America, in particular early Motown label songs it had cult status in venues such as Wigan Casino, Blackpool Mecca, The Twisted Wheel in Manchester and The Torch in Stoke. One of the iconic records of the movement was **The Night** by Frankie Valli & The Four Seasons released in May.

FEBRUARY Make Me Smile by Steve Harley & Cockney Rebel was the first release by the re-invented band which was disbanded in 1974

MARCH The Bay City Rollers had 3 chart singles in this year, with **Bye Bye Baby** being the bestselling record of the year. The Scottish group from Edinburgh boosted not only record sales but also sales of anything tartan to the plaid hungry teenage fans!

JUNE I'm Not in Love by 10cc was a top ten hit for 7 weeks, but remained a firm romantic favourite for years afterwards

AUGUST The second bestselling single of this year was Rod Stewart's **Sailing**, which stayed in the chart for 4 weeks, and was also used as the theme for the television programme about the Royal Navy warship 'Ark Royal'.

SEPTEMBER Hold Me Close written and performed by singer and actor David Essex stayed at No1 for 3 weeks.

NOVEMBER American country music singer Glen Campbell released **Rhinestone Cowboy** which was hugely popular with both country and pop audiences.

DECEMBER In the depths of winter Demis Roussos hit he charts with **Happy to Be on an Island in the Sun.**

1954

Sporting Headlines

FEBRUARY The **Ice Dance Championships** in Oslo, Norway, was won again by the British pair: Jean Westwood and Lawrence Demmy, who are the current World and European Champions.

MARCH The **World Snooker Championship** final was held in Houldsworth Hall in Manchester, where Fred Davis beat Walter Donaldson from Scotland. Fred, and his older brother Joe have between them won the World title for snooker and billiards many times. Born in Chesterfield, Derbyshire the boys learned to play from an early age in the pub run by their parents.

APRIL The **Grand National** this year was won by Bryan Marshall on 'Royal Tan', trained by Vincent O'Brien. This was Marshall's 2nd consecutive victory at Aintree. Only 29 horses ran, but unfortunately there were four equine fatalities.

JUNE The 5th **FIFA World Cup Final** was played in Switzerland, where West Germany beat the favourites, Hungary 3 goals to 2. This World Cup series of matches saw the highest ever scoring match with 12 goals, when Austria beat the hosts, Switzerland 7-5.

JULY The 90th **British Golf Open** was held at Royal Birkdale, Southport. The winner was Peter Thomson, an Australian from Melbourne, who went on to win in 1955 and 1956, becoming the only golfer in the 20th century to win the title in 3 consecutive years.

AUGUST The **British Empire and Commonwealth Games** were held in Vancouver, British Columbia. It was in these games that the 'Miracle Mile' was run, when both Roger Bannister and John Landy both completed a race in under 4 minutes. England won the games overall with 67 medals in total; 23 gold, 24 silver and 20 bronze.

SEPTEMBER in New York City, Rocky Marciano retained his **World Heavyweight** title with an 8th-round knockout of Ezzard Charles, who became the only man to ever last 15 rounds against Marciano.

Peter Thompson, winner of the 1954 Open Golf

SPORTING EVENTS

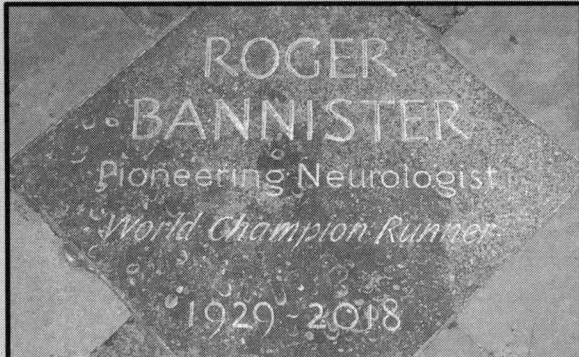

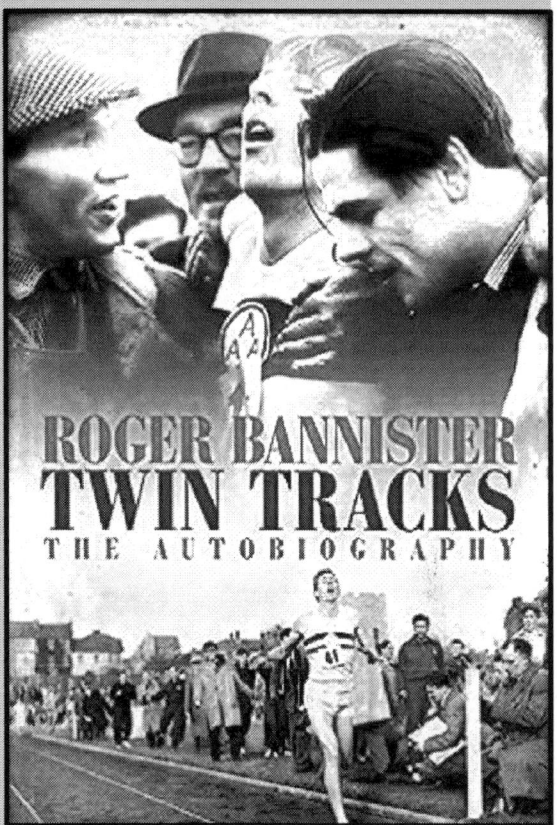

THE FIRST FOUR MINUTE MILE

Roger Bannister is one of those rare athletes who not only excelled on the world's competitive stage but became prominent in their chosen profession outside of sport. In May of 1954, he achieved his goal of running a mile in under 4 minutes, but at the end of the same year, retired from athletics altogether to concentrate on his work as a junior doctor and pursue his career in neurology. His love of running started at The City of Bath Boys School. Here he discovered a talent for cross country running winning the Junior cup three years in a row. He was eventually accepted to study medicine at Exeter College, Oxford, and started his running career in autumn 1946 at the age of 17.

His training regime was light, even compared to the standards of the day, plus he had never worn running spikes or run on a track before, but he showed promise. Although he was considered to be a possible entrant for the 1948 Olympic Games, he declined, preferring to wait 4 years to the 1952 games in Helsinki. During this time, he continued with his training programme of just 1 hour each day due to the pressure of his medical studies.

He came 4th in the 1500 metres and therefore didn't qualify for a medal, and subsequently decided on a much stricter regime of training to achieve his goal of being the first person ever to run a mile in under 4 minutes. On 6th May, 1954 at the Iffley Road Track, Oxford, with Chris Chataway and Chris Brasher as pacesetters, Chataway led until Bannister broke away in the last lap which he ran in 59 seconds. The historic final time was announced over the tannoy by Norris McWhirter, the publisher of The Guinness Book of Records as being 3 minutes 59.4 seconds.

1954

ROCK 'N ROLL

'**Rock Around the Clock**', released by Bill Haley and The Comets in 1954, is considered to be the song that brought rock and roll into mainstream culture around the world and became an anthem for the rebellious youth of the 1950's. It was the first rock & roll song to appear the following year in a film - Blackboard Jungle.

Originally from a poor background in Michigan, Haley left home with his guitar and very little else. Apart from learning how to exist on one meal a day, he worked at an open-air park show, sang and yodelled with any band that would have him, and worked with a travelling medicine show. He adopted his trademark kiss curl over his right eye to draw attention from his blind left eye, but it also became his "gimmick", and added to his popularity.

SEVEN YEARS IN TIBET

'**Seven Years In Tibet**' by Heinrich Harrer, Austrian mountaineer and Nazi SS sergeant, is an autobiographical book based on his experiences in Tibet during WWII and the interim period before the Battle of Chamdo in 1950, when the Chinese attempted to re-establish control over Tibet.

The book covers his escape from a British prisoner of war camp in India. Harrer travelled across Tibet to the capital Lhasa where he spent several years and subsequently became a tutor and friend of the 14th Dalai Lama, who at the beginning of the Flamingo edition of the book, says *'His book introduced hundreds of thousands of people to my country.'* It has been said that the book *'provided the world with a final glimpse of life in an independent Tibetan state prior to the Chinese invasion.'*

CULTURAL EVENTS

CHURCHILL'S BIRTHDAY PORTRAIT

Graham Sutherland painted a series of portraits of leading public figures, with those of Somerset Maugham and Lord Beaverbrook among the best known. In 1954 he was commissioned by Westminster to paint a portrait of Sir Winston Churchill to mark his 80th birthday.

A clash in their personalities greatly upset the sitter, who wanted to be depicted in a fictional scene in the robes of a Knight of the Garter, but Sutherland insisted on a realistic portrait in his morning suit, which depicted Churchill's solidity, strength and intransigent nature.

Despite initially refusing it, Churchill later accepted the painting describing it disparagingly as '*a remarkable example of modern art.*' However, it was never hung at his home, Chartwell, and was later destroyed by his private secretary with the approval of his wife, Clementine Churchill.

THE FUTURE ON TV

George Orwell's novel 1984 was transmitted by the BBC in December 1954. Viewers were shocked at the portrayal of a dystopian future, where media control, surveillance, and totalitarianism by the government demonstrate how a dictator can manipulate and control society in such a way that no one escapes. Here, the ruling party controls peoples' lives with the threat of the dreaded Room 101 as a punishment for disobedience.

MPs and press complained and the director, Rudolph Cartier, received death threats. This however only served to publicise the piece and when it was repeated days later, it drew the largest audience since the Coronation. The unforgettable performance from the young actor Peter Cushing who took on the central role of Winston Smith set him on the path to becoming one of cinemas iconic actors of the century.

1954

SYNTHETIC DIAMONDS

In December 1954, the scientist Herbert Strong, set up an experiment using a carbon and iron mixture with 2 small natural diamonds to 'seed' new diamond crystal growth. Using the application of high temperature and extreme pressure, the experiment was left running overnight, resulting in the carbon/iron mixture fusing into a blob. This was sent to the metallurgy department for polishing but they found that it couldn't be polished as it was so hard it was destroying the polishing wheel!

They subjected the fused material to further x-ray tests which confirmed from the crystalline structure that manufactured diamonds had in fact been made in the laboratory. Synthetic diamonds are now widely used in industry as abrasives in cutting and polishing tools, at a fraction of the cost of the natural stones.

An earth mined diamond

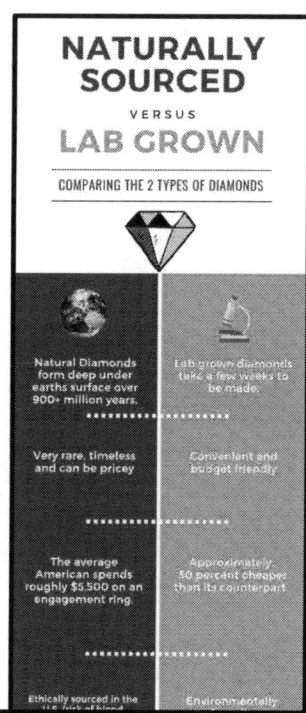

POLIO VACCINE

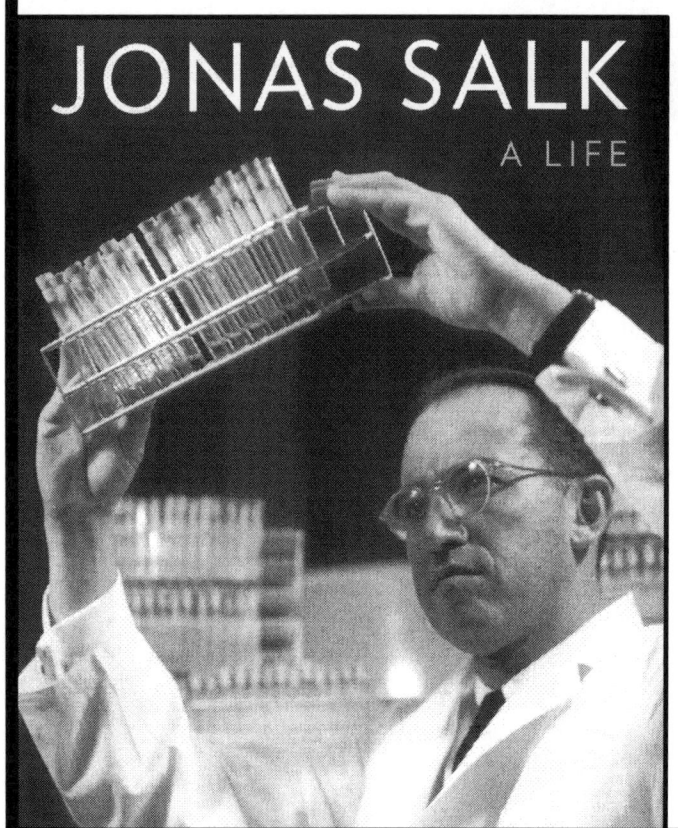

Polio or infantile paralysis is a highly infectious disease, mostly affecting young children, that attacks the nervous system, can lead to paralysis and in some cases death. In 1954 there were over 38,000 cases recorded in America. Many who survived faced leg braces, crutches or wheelchairs, and some were confined to an 'iron lung', an artificial respirator invented specifically for polio patients.

Whilst working as the head of the Virus Research Lab at The University of Pittsburgh, Jonas Salk, an American doctor discovered and perfected the first safe, effective vaccine against polio. After preliminary tests on laboratory animals, Salk tested his vaccine on children, and nearly 2 million 'polio pioneers' were injected in 1952/53, and in 1954 his vaccine was approved to begin the mass inoculation of children.

SCIENCE AND NATURE

CASPIAN TIGERS IN DANGER

In 1954 the last Caspian, or Persian Tiger, was killed in Turkmenistan. Elsewhere in Iran, Azerbaijan, central Asia, Afghanistan, Northwest China and the area around the Caspian sea, numbers have dwindled to single figures, and sightings are becoming less frequent.

The decimation of numbers has been blamed on excessive hunting for sport, especially in areas which have been colonised by the Russians since the 19th century. Also, their natural habitat, which is marshy reed beds, is being systematically cleared into fields for cotton production. The Caspian Tiger is stockier than the Siberian tiger and has a broader head. The fur also is much brighter in colour, and the black markings are narrower and more closely grouped, found on the head, neck, central back and the tip of the tail.

UNDERWATER EXPLORATION

Jacques Cousteau and his divers were commissioned in 1954 by the oil company British Petroleum to carry out a detailed and intensive survey of the waters around Abu Dhabi, the Persian Gulf and The Red Sea. Cousteau's ship, 'The Calypso', was used for the mission, but the remaining expenses were funded from the sale of his wife's expensive jewellery, such was the level of her support for his work.

It was during this period that the small submersible that was used for deep water filming and exploration was developed. The team shot over 25 kilometres of film over the 2 years they spent exploring the areas, 2.5 kilometres of which was used in a documentary film entitled **The Silent World**. When the film was shown at Cannes Film Festival in 1956 it won the Palme D'Or award for the best film.

1954 LIFESTYLES OF

During 1954 very few people had a television and the wireless reigned supreme. Daytime programmes were for wives, mothers and their children. 'Workers Playtime' continued to "come to you from a factory somewhere in England" and singers were interspersed with the major comedians of the day, Arthur Askey, Tommy Trinder, Charlie Chester and Ted Ray.

Music was important, with 'Music while you work' and 'Housewives Choice'. Soap operas gripped us, 'Mrs Dale's Diary' and 'The Archers'. Sunday lunchtimes meant 'Two-Way Family Favourites', music and messages for the troops in Germany. On Saturday evening we could "Stop the roar of London's mighty traffic" and listen to 'In Town Tonight', and the children weren't forgotten, they had 'Listen with Mother', Children's Hour 'Children's Favourites' with Uncle Mac.

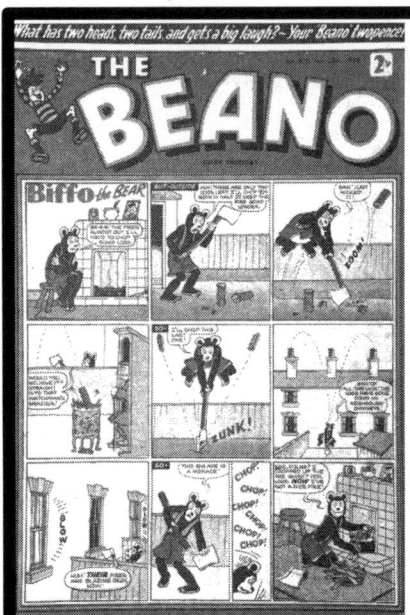

Sweet rationing had ended and happy children with a few pennies pocket money could choose sweeties from the rows of jars on the shelves. Four blackjacks or fruit salads for a penny, a Barratt's Sherbet Fountain with a stick of liquorice in it, raspberry drops, dolly mixture or toffees. You could 'smoke' a sweet cigarette whilst reading Dan Dare's adventures in Eagle or laugh with Radio Fun, Beano and Dandy comics.

EVERYDAY PEOPLE

The drabness of the war years gave way by 1954 to an age of colour and plastic in the home. Textile restrictions had been lifted and consumers were eager for new brightly patterned curtains and upholstery, and in the kitchen there were new coloured plastic goods.

G Plan furniture arrived. This new modular system was a range of modern furniture for the entire house which could be bought piece-by-piece according to budgets and individual room arrangements.

In 1954 the nuclear family was the norm, father out at work and mother busy with the housework. Less than 10% of households had a refrigerator, meat was stored in a wire mesh 'safe' in the larder,

vegetables wilted on a rack and shopping was done daily. It was the time of spam fritters, salmon sandwiches, tinned fruit with evaporated milk and ham salad for high tea on Sundays. Salad in the summer consisted of round lettuce, cucumber and tomatoes, and the only dressing available was Heinz Salad Cream, olive oil only came in tiny bottles from the chemist for your ears!

Many housewives wanted a Kenwood Chef to make baking and food preparation easier. And these new domestic inventions coincided with an upsurge in 'do-it-yourself' or DIY from the mid-1950s. The nation that had adopted a 'make do and mend' attitude during wartime privations took very readily to the idea of improving their homes themselves.

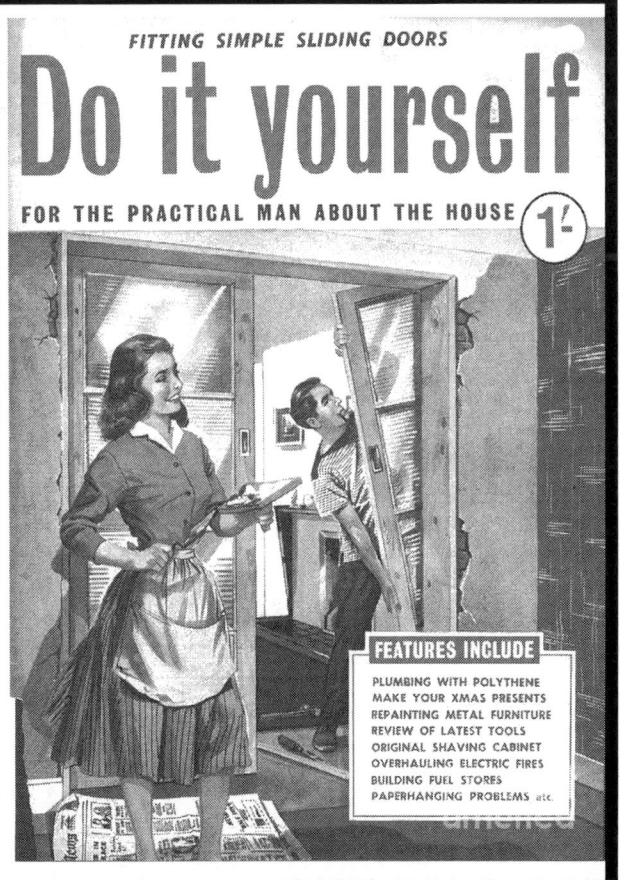

23

January 1st – 7th 1954

IN THE NEWS

Friday 1st — **"New Year Revels"** Huge crowds in London saw in the New Year with balloons and fireworks. Many tried to climb the lampposts, which had been greased earlier in the day. The party atmosphere continued into the small hours.

Saturday 2nd — **"Masters' View"** The Assistant Masters' Association have been asked to consider possible strike action for better pay. But many teachers feel that it is distasteful for professional men to strike, and have rejected the proposals.

Sunday 3rd — **"British Traditions Only"** The recent fashion from America, for hanging Christmas wreaths on front doors has been criticised as being alien and funereal. British people should stick to displaying a decorated tree in the front window instead.

Monday 4th — **"The Jitterbug Diet"** Hot dogs, crisps, peanuts and fizzy drinks, popular with the young, is being blamed for problems in childbirth and poor child development, the Institute of District Nursing has warned.

Tuesday 5th — **"Footing the Bill"** The current rigid economy is making it impossible to subsidise school lunches except in cases of real hardship. A subsidised meal currently costs 9d per day, whereas the full price is 1s 4d (7p).

Wednesday 6th — **"Radiating Knowledge"**
A top scientist has advocated the use of mildly radio-active isotopes in 6th Form science lessons, so that the next generation of research workers would have a head start in working in this new industry.

Thursday 7th — **"The Lost Mine"** A council in the Bristol area have lost an old drift mine. Surveyors are anxious to locate it in case it compromises a new housing development but have so far drawn a blank despite extensive searches.

HERE IN BRITAIN
"Husband Material"

Girls today are becoming very particular about the men they want to marry. Many now resort to a marriage bureau in order to find a prospective husband. They no longer want factory or farm workers, miners or bus drivers who come home dirty and aren't glamorous enough.
Girls want their beaux to be tall, dark and handsome, good with children and animals, sporty but cultured, with a good sense of humour. He must be a professional, with at least a £1000 per annum salary.

AROUND THE WORLD
"Wolves in Winter"

Heavy snow is continuing to cause havoc in Italy. In the Northern mountains, the 6ft deep drifts have cut off many townships, and over 100 cars have been abandoned. However isolated villages are now being terrorised by hungry wild animals. Yesterday a woodcutter working near Perugia was attacked by two wolves. He managed to kill one with his axe, the beast weighing almost 120 lbs, before driving the other away, although he was severely mauled in the struggle. This is the fourth wolf to be killed in the area since the severe cold spell began earlier this winter.

MAPPING ANTARCTICA

The ice-breaker 'Kista Dan' set sail from Melbourne, Australia on Monday 4th January. On its way sailing to Antarctica. The scientists on-board are searching for a suitable site for Australia's first permanent research station. 'Krista Dan' is an ideal vessel for this task having a cargo hold large enough to carry not only many months' supplies, but also a light aeroplane for the early mapping and surveying work.

Amongst the 24 passengers is a group of ten scientists with 12 more support staff including an engineer, a cook, a radio operator, a medical officer, a geologist and a carpenter. The team's initial task is to build the research station, and start work immediately on surveying the area, making detailed studies of the wildlife and climate. They will work under the leadership of R.G.Dovers, the renowned Australian Polar explorer, who has been a surveyor on expeditions since 1947, to Heard and Macquarie Islands and Terre Adelie, in Northern Antarctica.

Once the research station has been established the team will remain there for 12 months, cut off from the outside world. Temperatures can drop as low as -104 degrees Fahrenheit during the winter months from March to October, when there is little, or no, daylight. Blizzards often last for days, with winds up to 60 mph. However in summer which brings almost 24 hours daylight, the team will spend much of their time working outdoors, collecting scientific and meteorological information.

Bob Dovers is also an expert husky trainer, and several dog-sled teams will be used to take men out on explorations. With no fresh food or running water, the men will have to rely on tinned and dried rations, using melted snow for washing and cooking. Once 12 months tour of duty is over, another crew will replace them to continue this adventurous and important research work.

January 8th - 14th 1954

IN THE NEWS

Friday 8 — **"Elementary Anniversary"** The B.B.C. celebrated the 100th birthday of Sherlock Holmes. The 'consultant detective' created in 1887 by Arthur Conan Doyle, was born in January 1854 according to the book 'His Last Bow'.

Saturday 9 — **"The Worm Turns"** Angry lugworm diggers in Norfolk have gone on strike for an extra shilling per 100 worms. Dealers in Yarmouth and Lowestoft currently pay only 2s for the worms which are a favourite fishing bait with anglers.

Sunday 10 — **"Air Disaster"** A BOAC Comet passenger jet plane making a scheduled flight from London to Singapore exploded and crashed into the sea off the Italian coast. All 35 passengers including 10 children lost their lives.

Monday 11 — **"Harrogate Toy Fair"** Now in its fourth year, 600 firms will be accommodated in the converted bedrooms of five hotels and buyers are expected to place over £2 million worth of orders for next Christmas.

Tuesday 12 — **"Bountiful Fish"** Lowestoft fishermen have reported increased catches of herring since they began fishing off the South coast of Eire, 500 miles from their home port. Despite low prices, the long trips are proving worthwhile.

Wednesday 13 — **"Queen in New Zealand"** Wearing her Coronation gown with a diamond and emerald tiara, Her Majesty opened a special session of the New Zealand Parliament, the first monarch to do so.

Thursday 14 — **"Black Thursday"** Two coalmen from Islington were jailed for 6 months for assaulting the TV knitting expert, James Norbury, at a West End club. They claimed he had made rude remarks about how they ate their spaghetti.

HERE IN BRITAIN

"Freedom for American"

An American, Mr. Putnam Eaton who is Managing Director of a meat importers in Smithfield Market has been presented with the freedom of the Worshipful Company of Butchers of the City of London, for his services to the British meat trade.
Started in 975 AD it is one of the oldest of the 110 City of London Livery Companies. The Company's current headquarters, built in 1884, at Butchers' Hall suffered bomb damage in both world wars was and previous halls have been destroyed by fires, including The Great Fire of London in 1666..

AROUND THE WORLD

"A United Europe"

Politicians from France, West Germany, Belgium, Italy, the Netherlands and Luxembourg, have begun discussions to investigate setting up a new international community which will be governed by and in the interests of the European people. The committee, who will look into both institutional and economic areas, must report back by the 15th of March, so that proposals can be put to the whole assembly at the end of the month. It is stressed that there is no intention to create a super-power but create a better cooperation between these neighbouring countries.

DICKENSIAN OFFICES

Offices in 1954 were often little better than in 1854

The 1948 Factories Act set out minimum standards for occupational safety, health and welfare for those working in British manufacturing industry. However the Government has not seem fit to apply such standards to our clerical workers, most of whom are young women. Some working conditions are appalling – cramped, freezing cold, damp, and poorly lit, often in damp basements or condemned buildings with reports of rat infestations in some offices, causing staff to resign.

Investigating, a newspaper reporter wrote *"Close to the Bank of England an eighteen-year-old typist last night finished another week's work in a glum attic office where the wintry air streams through a dirty, broken window. The only heating in this freezing room is a tiny one-bar electric fire. The only light comes from one dim, unshaded bulb. At a dismal desk the girl huddles over an ancient typewriter. She wears an overcoat, scarf and snow boots. Her face is blue and pinched, she has chilblained hands. She is one of the thousands of office girls in Britain today who work in slum conditions that would be illegal in any factory. Her employer, who spends less than an hour a day in his icy office, runs a shoestring one-man business."*

An 1950 investigation into office working conditions headed by Sir Ernest Gowers, stated that there should be separate lavatory facilities for men and women, and at least 47 square feet of working space for each employee. There should be a thermometer in every office, and the temperature should never fall below 67 degrees Farhenheit (20deg C). Windows must be cleaned regularly to ensure plentiful natural light, and supplementary electric lighting should be 'suitable and efficient'. Despite protestations of sympathy by the Home Secretary, the recommendations have still to be put into effect. In the meantime, office workers have to put up with positively 'Dickensian' situations. Many, including Union representatives are now angrily demanding that the Home Secretary address this situation urgently, but those calls appear to be falling on deaf ears.

January 15th – 21st 1954

IN THE NEWS

Friday 15 — **"A Tall Order"** Tilly, a 5-day old giraffe at Belle Vue Zoo in Manchester was granted membership of 'Topliners', a club for the very tall. At 6'3" she already more than qualified for her badge!

Saturday 16 — **"Key to Survival"** A new survival suit will soon be issued to lifeboat crews. The rubber suit is designed to maintain the body's temperature even in freezing winter conditions during sea rescues.

Sunday 17 — **"Mau Mau Leader Captured"** 'General China', the reputed commander of one of the two largest terrorist organisations in Kenya, a man feared by thousands of tribesmen as a ruthless leader, and ranking next in importance to Kimathi, the terrorist chief, was captured by a patrol of the 7th (Kenya) Battalion, The King's African Rifles.

Monday 18 — **"Ballet Fans Disappointed"** The Sadler's Wells ballet company, touring North America, has reached Washington where every seat was sold out and hundreds of people have been turned away on each of the four evenings.

Tuesday 19 — **"Freedom of The City"** Admiral Lord Mountbatten of Burma and Lady Mountbatten were honoured by the "town and gown" of Edinburgh by receiving the Freedom of the City.

Wednesday 20 — **"£5M Dock Opened"** The largest oil dock in Great Britain at Eastham at the entrance to the Manchester Ship Canal was opened after four years of construction.

Thursday 21 — **"Korea Prisoners Released"** 22,500 Chinese and North Korean prisoners who have refused repatriation were transferred to UN military custody, are to be released in the first hour of Saturday. The Communist's sent a further protest to the neutral nations' repatriation commission describing the decision to release the prisoners as 'illegal.'

HERE IN BRITAIN

"A Man's Home is His Castle"

An Indian restaurant owner has brought the country to the city by setting up a caravan in his fourth-floor flat-cum-office in Soho, London. The caravan has a grass carpet surrounding it, crazy paving leading to its entrance, and a painted country setting on its walls. He sleeps in it at night and is considering getting gramophone records of birds tweeting for when he wakes up.

Initially, people laughed at his idea, but his Irish friend who builds caravans in Cardiff was delighted and built a 'Leprechaun Special' for him. The 4-berth caravan with a rural view through the window cost £425.

AROUND THE WORLD

"What A Whopper!"

Claimed to be the world's largest, a haggis weighing 831lb was carried in procession down Madison Avenue, New York.

Cooked in Stirling, it was flown to the New York office of the British Travel Association ending the journey with the accompaniment of bag pipes and drums.

Three girls accompanied the haggis, the ultimate destination of which is a series of Scottish celebrations in New York, culminating on 25th January, when plans for the first international Burns festival, to be held in Scotland next year, will be announced.

THE MONTE CARLO RALLY

ABOVE - Entry #23 was a Daimler Conquest (UK license ORW 86), entered by driver Tommy Wisdom

LEFT - Entry #69 (and the winner) was a Lancia Aurelia B20, entered by Louis Chiron (driver, behind the wheel here, left in the picture) and co-driver Ciro Basadonna.

Over 400 cars will set out from eight locations in Europe - Athens, Glasgow, Lisbon, Monte Carlo, Munich, Oslo, Palermo and Stockholm, on the 24th Monte Carlo Rally, travelling day and night until they reach Monte Carlo four days later. The event is a "concentration rally" in which competitors drive to Monaco, where the rally then continues to a set of special stages.

From its inception in 1911 by Prince Albert I, the race was intended to demonstrate improvements and innovations in automobiles, as well as promoting Monaco as a fashionable tourist resort on the Mediterranean shore. One of the most famous special stages covers 31km from La Bollène-Vésubie to Sospel, or the other way around, over a steep road with many hairpin bends. It passes over the Col de Turini, a mountain pass which normally has ice and snow on sections of it at that time of the year. Spectators also throw snow on the road to ensure that the conditions are suitably challenging for the cars! Thousands of fans watch the Turini stage, which due to the strong high beam lights cutting through the dark, is known as the 'Night of the Long Knives'.

Of the 21 nations represented, Britain has the largest number of entries with 121 cars competing of which Ford Zephyr is the most popular. Cars of French manufacture are the most numerous, totalling 157, of which 41 are Peugeots, the highest number of any single marque in the rally. The Italian contingent includes several high-quality cars of high, namely Lancias and Alfa-Romeos, whilst Germany boasts a high number of Porsches. The British contingent includes many drivers with the necessary skill and experience to win. Stirling Moss, who finished second last year, will start from Athens.

January 22ND - 28TH 1954

Friday 22   **"Going for Gold"** A gold-plated Jaguar car was among sixteen vehicles shipped from Liverpool en route to the New York Motor Show. It is the most prestigious annual event in the U.S. for the motor industry.

Saturday 23   **"House collapses"** A house purchased for £1 by Bristol Corporation, completely collapsed whilst being repaired. Workmen fled when the ceiling began to sag and managed to escape unharmed.

Sunday 24   **"Student Protests in Spain"** Madrid reports that nationalist students staged a demonstration outside the British Embassy to protest against the Queen's forthcoming visit to Gibraltar.

Monday 25   **"Posthumous Broadcast"** The first broadcast of Dylan Thomas's radio play 'Under Milk Wood' starring Richard Burton, was aired on the BBC Third Programme, just 2 months after the author's death.

Tuesday 26   **"East and West Differences"** The four Power conference opened with western speakers emphasising that the conference should concentrate on Germany and Austria with Russia pressing for agreement to hold a five-Power conference, to include China.

Wednesday 27   **"Last Resort"** County Councils are considering the possibility of just stopping the rent from the wages of tenants who are in arrears, to avoid evictions and the rising cost of welfare housing.

Thursday 28th   **"Spoiled Rotten"** American kids are being pampered too much by indulgent parents, a child study has warned. Many are failing to achieve the minimum standards of physical and mental ability.

HERE IN BRITAIN

"Beau Geste"

Children at a Lancashire Primary School were donating pennies for a lovely surprise, and speculating amongst themselves as to what it would be. Eventually the caretaker led a real seaside donkey through the gates, and the headmistress explained that their pennies had saved its life.

The donkey has been called "Beau Geste" because of the kind gesture which had saved him. Two local contractors have since put up the £18 purchase price, so the childrens' pennies will be used to pay for his keep, and the donkey will stay in the school grounds where the children will feed and groom him.

AROUND THE WORLD

"Australia's Role"

Much discussion is taking place amongst politicians in Australia as to its real position within the Commonwealth. They believe that Britain must abandon the habit of presenting policies for acceptance or rejection without due consultation.

Robert Menzies, the Prime Minister addressed words of pointed reproach when he said he was *"far from satisfied that we have the best machinery of consultation"* and that improvement from the United Kingdom end was needed. There have been occasions when ministers have read in newspapers of decisions affecting them before Whitehall has even sent the relevant information.

THE NAUTILUS

USS Submarine Nautilus was launched in Connecticut, on 21st January by Mrs Maimie Eisenhower. Possibly the most lethal warship ever devised, it is hoped it will be a symbol of man's mastery over the atom for peaceful purposes, it is the result of a pioneering effort which began five years ago. Weighing more than 3,000 tons she is a heavyweight, and though she is already in the water, her engines are not operational, as the nuclear reactor which will power them was too heavy for the launch slipway and will be inserted later into her hull. Nautilus is the first vessel to be propelled by atomic power, and she marks the beginning of a new chapter in the history of sea power. She is the world's first true submersible, which means that she can operate independent of the atmosphere above the sea's surface.

There was a sense of historical significance among the large crowd of dignitaries and guests, who attended the ceremony at the shipyards of the General Dynamics Corporation on the north shore of the River Thames, Connecticut. Her hull, painted a deep green, is rounded rather than streamlined, and at the stern each fin is fitted with a propeller. She will be able to cruise submerged indefinitely, and only the stamina of the crew will govern the time she stays underwater. Her speed will be more than 20 knots, with the capability to circumnavigate the globe without refuelling. The submarine reactor will use the same material that was the core component of the first atomic bomb, Uranium 235. Rear-Admiral Hyman Rickover, who was responsible for the production of the submarine, will now devote his attention to the construction of atomic power plants for cities.

JAN 29TH - FEB 4TH 1954

IN THE NEWS

Friday 29 — **"The Big Freeze"** Arctic conditions affected 14,000 miles of UK"s main roads. Snow will persist, but all-year-round swimmers at Salisbury's open-air baths braved the ice and swam as usual.

Saturday 30 — **"The Royal Tour"** The royal liner Gothic sailed from the little port of Bluff in New Zealand to the sound of a Maori farewell song. The Queen and the Duke of Edinburgh now cross the Tasman Sea to Australia.

Sunday 31 — **"Wasted"** Isle of Man grocers are throwing rotten eggs away by the dozen because although the current glut of eggs affects all of Britain, the island's law states they can't be sold at less than 6d (2.5p) per dozen.

Monday Feb 1 — **"Fond Farewell"** The 06.52 left Ingleton Station in Yorkshire for the last time yesterday, after 93 years. Over 100 passengers and a brass band made the farewell journey in three special coaches.

Tuesday 2 — **"Tots Away!"** The Australian Navy took over the escort of the Royal Yacht and the Queen sent the traditional signal to "Splice the Mainbrace". This means, an extra tot of rum for all the ship's company.

Wednesday 3 — **"Royal Scot Derailed"** Two coaches of the Royal Scot left the track just north of Watford Junction and the track was damaged for nearly 2 miles north of the station, and the main line was blocked in both directions.

Thursday 4 — **"New Element"** The Atomic Energy Commission announced that a new radioactive element, Number 99, has been produced. So far it is being known as 'ekaholmium'.

HERE IN BRITAIN

"Time Flies!"

According to the national chairman of the Fancy Goods Association it is now more difficult to sell badly designed fancy goods and furnishings, as the public have been strongly influenced by well decorated rooms shown in plays on television and in films on the cinema screen.

One item which is coming back into fashion, is the cuckoo clock, traditionally made in the Black Forest area of Southern Germany. He said that 50 years ago seven or eight tons of cuckoo clocks were brought into Britain each week, and that current imports are rising towards that figure again

AROUND THE WORLD

"Token Weight"

The ceremony of weighing the Aga Khan, the spiritual leader of the Ismaili Muslim sect, was held in Karachi to mark his 70th jubilee. Traditionally the wealthy would give the weight of the leader in jewels or precious metals as a thanks offering for their service and the leader would then use this tribute to fund charitable and philanthropic projects to benefit the people. This year however, the weighing will be symbolic with 1oz of platinum for every 141lbs of weight. The Aga Khan has asked that there should be no unnecessary expenditure in present economic conditions.

A Royal Home From Home

This passenger lounge was converted to be the Queens private lounge

The SS Gothic flying the Royal Ensign on the prow.

The liner "Gothic", in which the Queen and the Duke of Edinburgh are sailing on their tour of the Commonwealth has accommodation just as it was when "Gothic" had sailed in 1952 for the royal tour which was cancelled because of the death of King George VI.

The personal state rooms for her Majesty and the Duke of Edinburgh are situated aft on the level of the boat deck. Immediately below, on the promenade deck level, the smoking room has been partitioned to provide the Queen's day cabin on the starboard side and the Duke of Edinburgh"s day cabin on the port side. The Queen's day cabin has off-white walls, pale turquoise curtains and silver wall lights. The settee suites are covered with unglazed chintz. The Duke of Edinburgh's day cabin contains a mahogany writing desk used by Queen Victoria in the royal yacht "Victoria and Albert". Both day cabins are carpeted in dove grey, and each has an oxidised silver fireplace. In the lobby forward of the central vestibule is an illuminated wall map on which the route of the tour is traced in coloured light and on which the ship's position on any day can be shown. The veranda cafe immediately aft the day cabins will be used as a veranda by the Queen and the Duke of Edinburgh and is furnished with oak tables and chairs upholstered in blue and dark red .

On the saloon deck the dining saloon has been divided and now consists of the royal dining cabin on the starboard side and the lounge has been similarly divided. The 45ft royal barge is stowed in the after well-deck and is that used by King George VI during his tour of South Africa in 1947.

February 5th - 11th 1954

IN THE NEWS

Friday 5 — **"No Prejudice"** The renewal of a Manchester publican's license has been turned down on the grounds that the publican was alleged to have refused to serve a customer from Africa's Gold Coast.

Saturday 6 — **"Atom Fast Reactor at Work"** Zephyr, the zero-energy fast reactor at Harwell, went into operation yesterday. This is the first fast reactor to be built in the United Kingdom.

Sunday 7 — **"After the Thaw the Floods"** There was a thaw in all parts of Britain but many places had heavy snow or rain later, making road surfaces bad. In the north the slush froze again and the Automobile Association advised motorists going anywhere between the south coast and the Grampians because of widespread ice-bound conditions.

Monday 8 — **"Skivers?"** Reports suggest that there are increasing numbers of young men who are now using the influence of wealth or privilege to gain exemption from National Service.

Tuesday 9 — **"Coke Control Abolished"** The Minister of Fuel and Power announced that as stocks were now at record level, the public can now buy as much as coke as they like.

Wednesday 10 — **"600m Tons of Peat"** The Scottish Peat Committee have reported that full development of all the major peat lands might provide employment for 20,000 people for 100 years, mainly in the Highland counties.

Thursday 11 — **"Prone Pilot Jet Flight"** The first British jet aircraft to be flown by a pilot lying in the prone position, the "Prone Pilot Meteor" made its maiden flight yesterday. The aircraft, an adapted night fighter version of the Meteor interceptor, made a 28-minute flight.

HERE IN BRITAIN

"Kerbside Spies"

Hundreds of children in the Midlands have volunteered to become roadside "spies" for the Ministry of Transport's road research laboratory. The children, who are members of junior accident prevention councils, will work in pairs on various roads to count the number of motorcyclists wearing crash helmets and also record the weather.

The information gathered will be used by experts to study road safety. The Midlands organiser of the Royal Society for Prevention of Accidents applauded the children's participation and their important role in accident prevention.

AROUND THE WORLD

"Little Bombers"

Germany's smallest car, a midget three-wheeler, is being made by Messerschmitt who designed fighter planes for Hitler's Luftwaffe. Its point size makes it a popular option for urban life.

With an air-cooled engine and at 125 miles per gallon, it is certainly an economical vehicle. It shares many features found in aircraft design - the two seats are placed one behind the other, rather like the pilot and gunner in small fighter planes in the last war. You also get in and out of the car by lifting up the transparent hood.

Cost? A mere £240.

MILITARY PRECISION

Nearly 800 officer cadets displayed impeccable precision at the 19th Sovereign's Parade held recently at The Royal Military Academy, Sandhurst. In a forthright address, Field Marshall Lord Tunis spoke of the tasks with which the cadets would be confronted when they joined their units and spoke of the qualities of a good officer, who would never ask his men to carry out orders which he himself would not be prepared to undertake. The cadet must be willing to get to know his men, their strengths and weaknesses, but at the same time be strict and impartial in ensuring that orders were carried out. He must always exercise complete self-discipline, ensuring that his own conduct is always above reproach thus setting a good example to his men.

Located in Berkshire, Sandhurst is one of several military academies of the United Kingdom and is the British Army's initial officer training centre. Prior to its founding, most British Army officers received professional training at privately run military colleges but in 1802 The Military Academy was opened with the aim of being *"the centre of national excellence in officer training"*.

Three Sovereign's or "Passing Out" parades are held each year, with senior cadets Trooping the Colours past the Sovereign and guests, including the graduating cadets' families and friends. Various awards are presented to cadets who have displayed particular excellence in various disciplines during their training. The Sword of Honour is awarded to the Officer Cadet considered to be the best of his particular intake, while The Queen's medal is awarded to the Officer Cadet who has achieved the best overall results in military, academic and practical studies. Such is the reputation of the Academy that it now attracts cadets from all over the world.

February 12th - 18th 1954

IN THE NEWS

Friday 12 — **"Last Word"** A workman employed on the Old Chancery in 1945 came across Adolf Hitler's Will, dated 1938. The electrician's widow has now put the document up for auction in Berlin.

Saturday 13 — **"No Proof"** The Government has accepted the report of the Standing Advisory Committee on Cancer stating *"there is no proof that smoking is a cause of lung cancer."*

Sunday 14 — **"Films for the Forces"** The Army is to purchase three cinemas on Salisbury Plain, and civilians will no longer be admitted. Residents in nearby villages, some of whom have used the cinemas for 30 years or more, have expressed resentment at the decision.

Monday 15 — **"Saving Historic Buildings"** Buildings on a list of historic or architectural interest qualify for a grant of £250,000 a year for repair and maintenance and £500,000 a year for 5 years for the purchase of outstanding buildings.

Tuesday 16 — **"Birmingham Ballot"** In a recruitment drive, Birmingham City Transport and the General Workers Union are asking their members for a straight answer to the question, *"Have you any objection to the department employing coloured workers."*

Wednesday 17 — **"Record Descent in Atlantic"** Two French naval officers beat the world record for an ocean descent when the naval bathyscaphe in which they had enclosed themselves reached a depth of 13,287ft. off the coast of Dakar.

Thursday 18 — **"Submarines for Sale"** Two fully equipped submarines are for sale in Antwerp Harbour for £35 the pair. Both are advertised as being in good running order.

HERE IN BRITAIN

"Final Move"

The famous clipper "Cutty Sark" has returned to the East India Dock in London. She was towed down river by the two tugs "Gondia" and "Java" who then spent an anxious hour moving the ship across the dock basin and through a lock to a temporary berth, where she will be examined carefully to determine what remedial work needs to be done to stabilise her.

This will take possibly up to 12 months before she can be taken to her final resting place at Greenwich where she will be preserved for posterity. The Preservation fund currently stands at £170,000, with a further £80,000 still needed.

AROUND THE WORLD

"Stamp Sale"

Prince Farouk's private collection of stamps was put up for auction in Cairo recently, attracting bidders and collectors from all over the world. An avid collector of many things, the Prince had also amassed one of the greatest collections of Egyptian stamps in the world.

When he abdicated in favour of his son, during the 1952 Egyptian revolution and fled to Monaco, he left most of his possessions and valuables behind in his haste.

The stamp collection which was estimated at a value of £100,000 realised a total of £135,675. Almost £90,000 of the bids were paid in cash.

IDEAL HOME FURNISHINGS

Earls Court was the venue for the fifth British Furniture Exhibition since the war. With nearly 300 British exhibitors on display, the consumer had ample opportunity to compare the merchandise and give their comments directly to the retailers. Utility furniture was produced in the United Kingdom during and directly after World War II under a government scheme which was designed to cope with raw material shortages and usage. Introduced in 1942, the Utility Furniture Scheme continued into post-war austerity and lasted until 1952. Until then, new furniture was restricted to newly married couples or those whose homes had been destroyed by bomb damage, and now, many people are taking the opportunity to refresh their homes with new designs.

Since the elimination of the Utility scheme, many new furniture ideas have been developed and will be showcased for the first time at Earls Court. Foam rubber has made possible clean and lightweight furniture designs that maintain comfort and whilst the trend on the continent seems to favour the more angular and outlandish designs of modern art. The British public have a more restrained taste, with much plainer finishes in fabric, design and ornamentation being the order of the day. Floors too have undergone a transformation with flecked or plain carpets proving more popular than the ornate, heavily patterned ones of pre-war years. The latest rubber backed floor coverings produced by a needle loom process are gaining in popularity over the cheaper varieties of carpet, although the more expensive Wilton and Axminster carpets are still the first choice for those who can afford them.

The recent changes in building regulations for housing has also had an effect on the interior design industry. Rooms are becoming smaller, and multi-functional, so the pieces we use to furnish those rooms will need to reflect these changes.

February 19th - 25th 1954

IN THE NEWS

Friday 19 — **"Royal Exhibition"** An exhibition of silver gilt from the Royal Palaces opened at the Victoria and Albert Museum. Pieces from the 17th to early 19th Centuries are on display.

Saturday 20 — **"Last Voyage"** The oldest ship in the P&O fleet, and the first to exceed 20,000 tons, the liner Maloja, ended her last voyage. She entered service in 1923 mainly between Britain and Australia, but in WW2 served as an armed merchant cruiser and as a troopship.

Sunday 21 — **"ICI Need £30m"** The company is to raise the largest amount of fresh funds asked for at one time since the war to fund the expansion of, among other projects, the production of Terylene and titanium.

Monday 22 — **"Royal Children to Join the Queen"** The Duke of Cornwall and Princess Anne will sail in the Royal Yacht Britannia to Tobruk via Malta and Gibraltar, to make the homeward journey with the Queen and Duke of Edinburgh on the final stages of the royal tour.

Tuesday 23 — **"Monte Carlo Winner"** Louis Chiron, of Monaco, who drove a 21 litre Lancia, was officially confirmed as winner of the Monte Carlo rally. Protests that his car had a more powerful engine than that fitted by the manufacturers, were dismissed.

Wednesday 24 — **"Speed Trials"** A French locomotive has just completed 3 days of speed trials achieving a speed of 150 mph while pulling three full passenger coaches. This beats the previous record by 7 mph.

Thursday 25 — **"New Premier"** Lt. Col Abdel Nasser who led the revolution in Egypt in 1952, has become the new premier of Egypt following the resignation of General Naguib.

HERE IN BRITAIN

"Daily Pint"

The demand for milk in Britain has been falling because a wider choice of food has been available, and more milk has been used in the production of cheese. The present trend is for consumers to take less fat, and the dairy industry is now obliged to offer low fat and even skim milk.

The Milk Marketing Board is anxious to maintain and possibly increase the demand for liquid milk, which by far offers the most profitable market. To this end they have been looking at the industry in America, where they found that the costs involved in production and distribution are lower than in Britain.

AROUND THE WORLD

"Hidden Costs"

There has been much debate and heated discussion in the Eastern Nigeria House of Assembly, where the rising cost of brides is causing consternation. According to Islamic tradition in several African countries, the groom will pay a sum of money to the bride's father. If the bride price is not paid in full, the wedding doesn't take place.

The amount owed is negotiated between the male members of both families and can be paid in cash or in cattle or a combination of both. However, it seems that currently more and more marriageable girls are going to the highest bidder.

Queen Mary's Gifts

The Coronation of King George V

Queen Mary's coffin

Thirteen coins from the personal effects of Queen Mary have been given by the Princess Royal to the Westminster Abbey appeal fund who may decide to have them mounted and offered for sale. The Princess Royal explained that the coins had been given to Queen Mary by servants in return for presents of knives and scissors in accordance with the custom that one must give something in return for the gift of a cutting instrument. An exhibition of Queen Mary's art treasures is to be shown at the Victoria and Albert Museum. It will include furniture, porcelain, jades, snuff boxes, ivories, and enamels plus some of Queen Mary"s dresses and examples of her needlework.

Queen Mary was born Victoria Mary Augusta Louise Olga Pauline Claudine Agnes Mary in Kensington Palace in 1867 to Duke Francis and Duchess Mary of Teck. Young Mary, known as May, is the great-granddaughter of George III and a second cousin to Queen Victoria. At the behest of Queen Victoria, Mary was engaged to Queen Victoria's grandson Prince Albert Victor but he died shortly afterwards. Queen Victoria suggested that Mary marry Albert's brother George and although it was an arranged marriage, it was plain to see that George and Mary became deeply in love. When Queen Victoria died, Mary's father-in-law became King Edward VII and when he died, George became King George V and Mary his Queen. The King and Queen were married at Westminster Abbey on April 26, 1923.

Queen Mary devoted herself to many charities, but also liked to collect jewels and she was known for wearing several dazzling pieces of jewellery all at one time. She might wear several necklaces, brooches, stomachers, bracelets, rings and of course a crown, often mixing diamonds, pearls, emeralds, sapphires and rubies.

Feb 26th - March 4th 1954

IN THE NEWS

Friday 26 — **"Senior Service"** Over 8,000 men who entered the Royal Navy on post war engagements are due for release, but neither the Navy nor The Royal Marines have sufficient new recruits to replace them.

Saturday 27 — **"Arsenal Scheme Adopted"** A plan for the restoration and reorganisation of the Woolwich Arsenal has been adopted. Every effort is to be made not to cause hardship to the worker and any job losses will be brought about by normal wastage.

Sunday 28 — **"Three Days of Prayer"** The Catholics of Rome began three days of prayer for their bishop, the Pope, in his illness. The special services in St. Peter's will end on the fifteenth anniversary of the Pope's election on the eve of his seventy-eighth birthday.

Mon 1 March — **"C of E Protest"** Members of the Church of England have been asked to protest to the BBC, over plans to televise the canonisation ceremony of Pope Pius XII this summer.

Tuesday 2 — **"Croydon's Claim"** Croydon is to petition the Queen for city status. The award will be a boost to the town's civic pride as Croydon is the only county borough with a population exceeding 200,000 which does not have such status.

Wednesday 3 — **"Good Works"** A Grimsby vicar has plans to get his church cleaned in Lent and will hand out buckets and scrubbing brushes to female parishioners. "*It will be good for them spiritually*," he said.

Thursday 4 — **"Power for the National Grid"** A breeder reactor to be built at Dounreay will be Britain's second atomic power station. The construction of the plant will require about 2,000 workmen and take several years.

HERE IN BRITAIN

"Butter Battles Commence"

The date for de-rationing butter and margarine is approaching and manufacturers are busily developing a new super-margarine that will rival butter in taste. They are spending millions of pounds to achieve their goal, but if they are successful, the rewards will be rich indeed. The new super margarines will contain the sunshine vitamins A and D which were compulsorily added at the beginning of the war. However, the butter producers are fighting back. They are experimenting with foil packaging for both "Salted" and "Natural" butter to extend the keeping qualities of their product.

AROUND THE WORLD

"The Truth Box"

Firms in America are turning to a new device in the battle against theft. It looks like a harmless suitcase and costs about £450. The lie detector has been used for years by the police, but never before in industry. Flexible leads extend from the machine, one wrapped around the hand measures the perspiration in your palm and another goes round your arm, recording blood pressure. A third is wrapped round your chest and measures how fast you breathe. They leads are connected to three pens, which draw onto a coil of paper, your body's reactions while you're being questioned.

New Towns

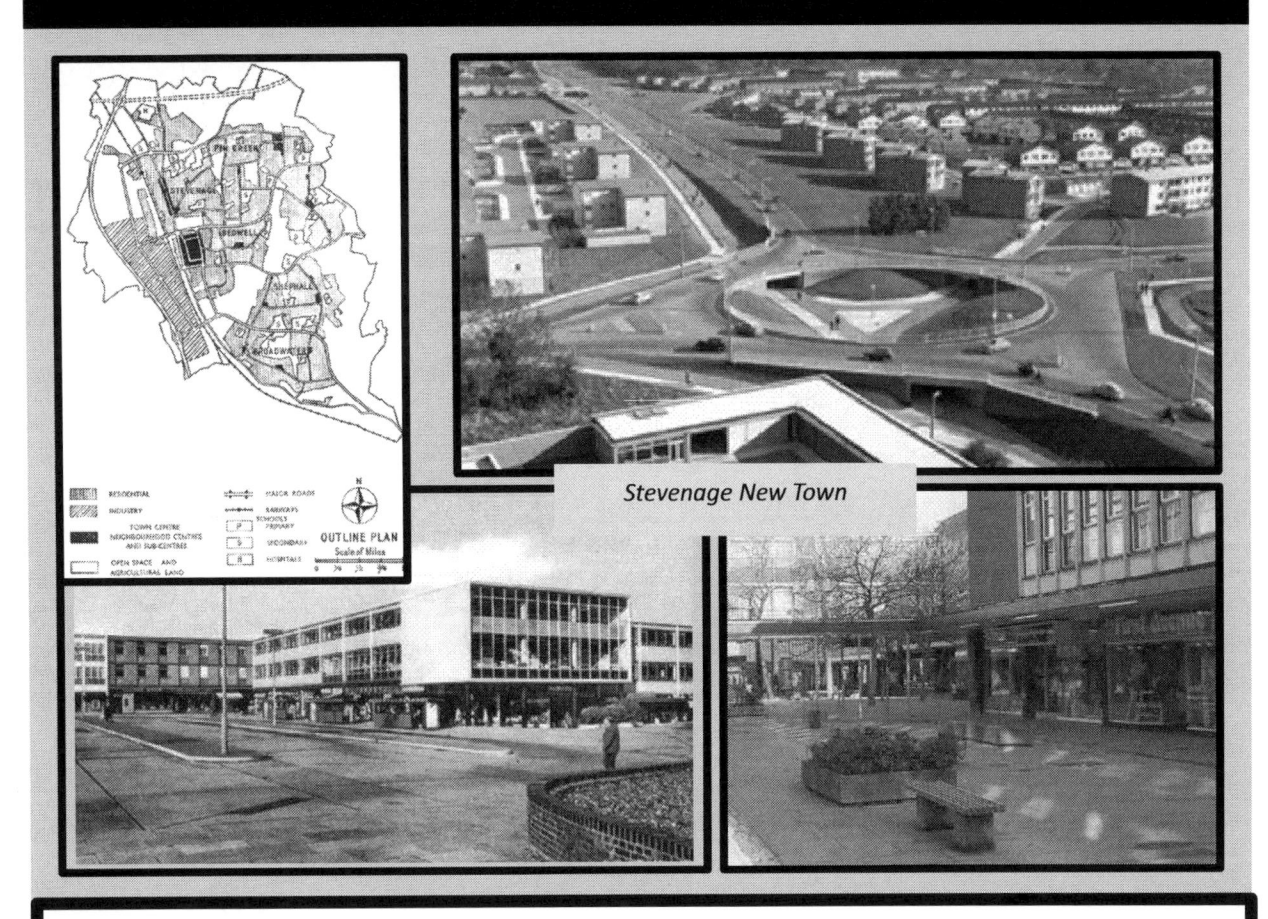

Stevenage New Town

Britain's new towns are springing up across the land - modern, visionary, and clean. There is no gradual expansion or urban sprawl, as these towns have been meticulously designed and planned on paper, mathematically calculated to deliver the right amount of space per person, roadway and parking per car, and facilities for the consumer. Schools, surgeries and cinemas have been included, crèche facilities, shopping centres, pedestrian access ways, all designed and thought out to the last degree.

The population was already pushing some towns and cities to bursting point before the war, but the ravages of the blitz has rendered many people homeless, some sharing crowded accommodation with parents or being housed in temporary pre-fabricated buildings. These new towns built in the best British countryside are desperately needed where there are factories and offices to provide employment for the new residents. There will be road and rail connections to service them and link them with the rest of the country. Sewage and water systems, planned meticulously, will connect to the existing network of underground pipes and reservoirs and, powered by clean electricity and gas, every home and every workplace will benefit from all that modern conveniences promise.

This is not just visionary but is already happening now in places like Stevenage in Hertfordshire, Harlow in Essex, Corby and Milton Keynes in Northamptonshire. As the first phases of construction are completed, people are starting to move away from the damaged and overcrowded areas of the country, building new communities in the process. The benefits to the economy will far outweigh the developmental costs, as our working and living conditions are regenerated. This is the architects' and town planners' vision for our future.

March 5th - 11th 1954

IN THE NEWS

Friday 5 — **"Seabirds Destroyed"** More than 800 sea birds covered with thick black oil have been destroyed by the RSPCA along the 30 miles of coast from Perranporth to beyond Padstow.

Saturday 6 — **"Hydrogen Peroxide as Fuel"** The first submarine of post war design, 'Explorer', launched at Barrow-in-Furness by Vickers-Armstrong, is propelled by hydrogen peroxide fuel.

Sunday 7 — **"Valley to Become Reservoir"** Dwellings of 30 people in the Amber Valley in Derbyshire, will be submerged if proposals to flood 200 acres of land to provide a 1,300-million-gallon reservoir at a cost of £860,000, goes ahead.

Monday 8 — **"Comet's Return to Service"** BOAC is expected to resume services of their Comet aircraft which have been grounded since one crashed in the Mediterranean early in January. Modifications have been made to the aircraft since then.

Tuesday 9 — **"Miners' Strike Spreads"** About 3,500 South Shields miners from all but one pit in the area, are now idle because of grievances by the men against one "tyrannical" overman at Whitburn Colliery.

Wednesday 10 — **"Uniform Pay"** Nurses have complained to the Government of the cost of buying their own stockings and shoes. Women in the Police and armed forces are issued with these as part of their uniform.

Thursday 11 — **"Underground TV Station"** Britain's first underground television station is being planned at Crystal Palace. The aerial system - the only significant construction above ground - will be erected at the top of a self-supporting steel mast 640ft. high, thus giving an effective height of 1,000ft. above sea level and be more powerful than any other in the world.

HERE IN BRITAIN

"Good Eggs"

To promote sales of British eggs, now that rationing is over, there is a new initiative by poultry farmers in this country called "The Good Egg Club". During the war years, housewives became used to managing with one egg per person per week, but now thankfully that is a thing of the past.

The slogan of the campaign is *"I'm a good egg. I remind mother to buy eggs by the dozen each week."* Children are being encouraged to join up during Lancashire's annual Egg and Poultry Week and will be given an egg-shaped badge to wear.

AROUND THE WORLD

"Russian Elections"

The first elections in Soviet Russia since the death of Stalin a year ago are due to be held. More than 115 million men and women over the age of 18 are expected to take part, and to make certain that everyone goes to the polls, voting is held on a Sunday.

The voters are supposedly deciding on the election of the Supreme Soviet, however in reality, only one political party, the Communists, will be represented. Stalin famously stated, *"A party represents a class of society and where there is only one class there can be only one political party."*

DEATH OF AN EMPRESS

The burnt-out hulk of the cruise liner "Empress of Canada" was righted in Gladstone Dock, Liverpool where it has rested since early 1953, when the vessel caught fire and capsized. The whole operation was the third biggest of its kind to be undertaken since the raising of the Normandie, at New York in 1942, and of the American battleship Oklahoma, at Pearl Harbour. Sixteen cables were affixed to the starboard side of the ship, stretching to winches anchored in concrete. The liner will stay where she lies until made watertight for re-floating.

Originally launched as "The Duchess of Richmond" in 1928, she sailed on her maiden voyage from Liverpool a year later on a six-week cruise to the West Coast of Africa. Amongst her passengers then were the Chief Scout, Lt. General Sir Robert Baden-Powell, and his wife. On 14th February 1940 she began her distinguished war service when she was requisitioned as a troopship and left for Suez. During the invasion of North Africa, in December 1942, she sailed in convoy with other troop ships which were attacked by German U-boats, when several of the ships were sunk and many lives lost. In March 1945 she sailed to the Black Sea port of Odessa carrying 3,700 Russians who had been held prisoner in France and eight months later she sailed from Rangoon to Liverpool with the last of the prisoners-of-war from Sumatra and Singapore.

Refurbished and re-launched as The Empress of Canada in 1946 she completed 7 years' service again as a prestigious cruise liner, before sailing in to Liverpool for a routine winter overhaul. On 25th January, whilst lying in Gladstone No.1 Branch Dock, the "Empress" caught fire and, despite the tremendous efforts of firemen from all over the north-west of England, she eventually slid on her side along the dock bottom and became a burnt-out hulk.

March 12th - 18th 1954

IN THE NEWS

Friday 12 — **"Avalanche deaths"** Two young couples are the latest victims to be killed by avalanches on the mountain slopes of Austria this winter. The death toll this year has reached 150.

Saturday 13 — **"Film Workers Dismissed"** 2,000 workers in film laboratories whose union, the Association of Cinematograph and Allied Technicians, have refused to cancel a ban on overtime and work-to-rule tactics, have been given one week's notice.

Sunday 14 — **"Sold Out"** The BBC were dismayed to learn that their commentary of The Grand National will be sponsored by "Owbridge's Lung Tonic" when it is broadcast on South African Radio this year.

Monday 15 — **"Fatal Crash"** A British BOAC plane en route from Sydney to London burst into flames on landing at Kallang, Singapore. The death toll so far is known to be 33.

Tuesday 16 — **"Children Back to Old School"** The six remaining children at Sunbury-on-Thames, who have been on a school strike for 18 months, are being allowed by Middlesex County Council to return to the school from which their parents refused to transfer them in September 1952. Originally, 90 children were kept away from school, but many parents later withdrew their objections.

Wednesday 17 — **"Pollution Probe"** A demand has been made in Parliament for a speed-up of research into the part air pollution plays in causing disease. The Commons yesterday denounced this menace to public health.

Thursday 18 — **"Atomic Test"** The United States Government expressed grave concern over reports of Japanese fishing crews being injured during recent American atomic tests in the Pacific.

HERE IN BRITAIN
"Pudding Basin Cuts"

The National Federation of Hairdressers have recommended that 2s (10p) be the minimum price of a short back and sides, in order to meet rising costs. However, barbers in the Northeast are worried that the increased price will drive miners back to the old style "pudding basin" cuts performed by their wives at home.

They say that an increase of 6d (2.5p) on the price most barbers charge for a haircut is going too far, but an ex-president of The Federation thinks a regression unlikely as miners are now accustomed to having neatly trimmed hair.

AROUND THE WORLD
"Shy Voters"

Only 65% of possible voters turned out in the Karachi elections. The reason given was that Pakistani women aren't traditionally seen in public, and many in the poorer areas cannot afford a burqa which must be worn outside the home according to Islamic Law. The all-enveloping "modesty" garment covers the entire female body from head to toe, with only a mesh opening over the eyes.

There was also a problem with the required identification, and officials had to make do with a red ink stamp on the voters' hand to prevent repeat visits to the polling booth.

Pearl Fishing

The news that ten experienced sponge divers have gone to help with the Australian pearl diving season off the Darwin coast comes as a result of an investigation carried out last year when a special Australian emissary went to Athens to explore using sponge fishermen of the island of Kalymnos in the Aegean Sea as pearl divers. The 15,000 inhabitants of Kalymnos, a small, barren rock island, made their livelihood in the past almost exclusively from sponge fishing, but during the previous two years the trade had died, and the island was abandoned. On the other hand, Australia, has the world's largest and finest pearl shell beds on its northern borders, and before the war had a pearling fleet of about 300 luggers, manned mostly by Asians. Rather than readmit Japanese divers, they were looking for pearl divers among potential European migrants.

Two factors determined the practicability of the scheme, whether the Kalymnos fishermen were prepared to emigrate to Australia, and, whether they have or could acquire, the aptitude for pearl diving The Japanese pearl divers are able to descend to as much as 20 fathoms below the sea level, more than the Malays who can descend to only 12 to 14 fathoms. These ten Greeks will see for themselves the kind of life they would be expected to lead and the greater rigour of pearl diving as they will face quite a strenuous test. However, the experience of the Dodecanese fishermen who emigrated to the southern coast of Florida is taken as an indication that the men from Kalymnos stand a fair chance. For Australia, pearl shell has become a good source of revenue and in 1952 reached the unprecedented price of $A700 per ton. The occasional prize pearl, such as "Star of the West", valued at $A14,000, is, of course, an additional incentive.

March 19th - 25th 1954

IN THE NEWS

Friday 19 — **"Houses on HP"** Bedford Town Council has approved a plan which would allow tenants to buy their council houses on hire purchase and so avoid paying a large deposit.

Saturday 20 — **"Assembly Rooms Rebuild"** The National Trust announced that they will rebuild Bath Assembly Rooms exactly as they were before destruction by enemy action in 1942.

Sunday 21 — **"Three Bears at Large"** Three bears which had been appearing at a local theatre caused alarm when they took a stroll round Newcastle's shopping area. It is thought that one of them got a paw under a cage door, lifted it, and scrambled out.

Monday 22 — **"Gold Market Opened"** After being closed for more than 14 years, the London gold market re-opened. The Treasury stated that the market will work on a restricted basis, under the general supervision of the Bank of England.

Tuesday 23 — **"Long Distance Calls"** The Post Office has ordered the first of two transatlantic telephone cables that will be installed between Oban and Newfoundland.

Wednesday 24 — **"Temple Church Re-Dedicated"** The Temple Church, burnt out in the war, was re-dedicated by the Archbishop of Canterbury in the presence of Queen Elizabeth the Queen Mother. Her Majesty is a bencher of the Middle Temple to which, with the Inner Temple, the church jointly belongs.

Thursday 25 — **"Medical Tests for Drivers"** Suggestions to doctors on how to conduct medical examinations of persons suspected of being under the influence of alcohol, have been submitted by the British Medical Association. They believe several thousands of road accidents are caused by drink drivers, but official records show a much smaller number.

HERE IN BRITAIN

"Simpsons"

A reception was held at Simpson Services Club to welcome the visiting American "Jesters" squash rackets team, at the start of their tour. Simpson's is one of London's oldest traditional English restaurants famed for its traditional food, particularly roast meats which sadly are still restricted under rationing.

During the war Simpson's was severely hit by a shortage of butchers' meat, but partial relief came from generous agreements with some clients to supply game from their own estates. Simpson's, like all luxury restaurants, was included in the wartime rule imposing a five-shilling limit on the price of a restaurant meal.

AROUND THE WORLD

"The Movies"

British studios are experiencing an influx of Hollywood stars and producers who are seeking to escape the pressures of the big screen in America. While Hollywood once held the promise of lavish parties and mountains of money, the trend is now towards playing it safe with fewer movies being made due to fear of failure.

Many film goers still long for the substantial, old-fashioned movies of the past, which is leading to the migration of screen idols to Britain. This is a great compliment to British studios and their policy of making better, more substantial films rather than just bigger ones.

GRAND OLD LADY

Good progress is being made to recover metal from the wreck of the old battleship Warspite which now lies about 700ft. from high water mark off Marazion beach in Cornwall. All the steel that is brought back is sold to the British Iron and Steel Corporation but the problem of reclaiming so much scrap from the sea is still great. The original plan to re-float the battleship and tow her from the rocks in Mount's Bay to a shipbreaker's yard was frustrated when the wreck had to be beached, where, all but submerged, she has for months been "attacked" by divers using underwater cutting oxy-acetylene flames and explosives in an effort to split the ship in two.

Then the fore section was sealed and made watertight, and with the aid of compressed air from two jet aircraft engines it was floated towards the sands of Marazion. The after part of the ship was later treated in similar fashion and now the two sections lie in V-formation, ready for the final onslaught by the shipbreakers. Disaster came to the Warspite in April 1947, when she was being towed from Portsmouth to the Clyde for breaking up. A towrope parted during a gale off Lands End and the battleship was swept on to the rocks in Prussia Cove on the eastern shores of Mount's Bay.

HMS Warspite was a Queen Elizabeth-class battleship launched for the Royal Navy in 1913 She was deployed in WW1, served as a Flagship in the Atlantic and Mediterranean during the inter-war years and thoroughly modernised in the mid 1930s. She served in several campaigns in WW2, her actions earning her the most battle honours ever awarded to an individual ship in the RN. Warspite gained the nickname the 'Grand Old Lady' from Admiral Sir Andrew Cunningham in 1943 while she was his flagship.

March 26th - April 1st 1954

IN THE NEWS

Friday 26 — **"Last Chapter of Tour"** The Queen and the Duke of Edinburgh flew from Adelaide to Perth where an epidemic of polio meant an absence of handshaking, but there was no sign of any undue concern over the epidemic in the gay, crowded streets of Perth.

Saturday 27 — **"Grand National"** Large crowds attended the Grand National and Lancashire County Police used a helicopter at Aintree for the first time to help with traffic control.

Sunday 28 — **"Brighton Centenary"** Brighton celebrated the centenary of its incorporation as a borough with horse drawn hansom cabs, mounted guards parading in the uniform of 1854, and with policemen doing their modern duties in the dress of 100 years ago.

Monday 29 — **"Troopship Ablaze"** The troopship 'Empire Windrush', sailing to Britain from the Far East with more than 1,500 men, women, and children on board, was abandoned in the Mediterranean after fire had broken out in the engine-room. Four members of the crew perished and the survivors were later landed at Algiers.

Tuesday 30 — **"Stop Press"** The daily newspaper 'The Recorder', which began publication only last October, has closed down. Industrial action by printers has been blamed.

Wednesday 31 — **"Faithful Servant"** An elderly shepherd reported missing in December, has been found dead on the Peak District moors. His 12-year-old sheepdog had guarded the body through severe weather and heavy snowfalls.

Thurs April 1 — **"Parking Ban Near Crossings"** It will be an offence to park a vehicle within 45ft. of a zebra crossing under new regulations published by the Ministry of Transport. The lighting of beacons at these crossings will also be a legal requirement.

HERE IN BRITAIN
"Threat of Fire They Can't See"

The town of Tow Law in County Durham has a long history of mining, and the whole town is built on a labyrinth of workings, some of them long abandoned. This week, workmen have been pouring cement into a 20ft deep moat in a bid to check a fire that threatens to spread underneath the town.

The fire, smouldering in disused workings, is only three yards from some of the peoples' homes and those families in greatest danger have been evacuated. Children's bonfires on waste land are believed to have started the shale smouldering and the fire may have been spreading for months.

AROUND THE WORLD
"Conditions at Spandau"

Spandau Prison in West Berlin, which was originally a concentration camp under the Nazis, now houses seven leading German officers who were sentenced at Nuremberg for war crimes. The western Powers have been under pressure from the Federal authorities to secure improvements in the treatment of the prisoners and some small ones have been agreed, prisoners are now allowed one 30-minute visit every month instead of one fifteen-minute visit every two. The authorities also wish to prohibit warders switching on the lights in the cells at any time during the night to ensure that the prisoners are still there.

Long Lasting Prints

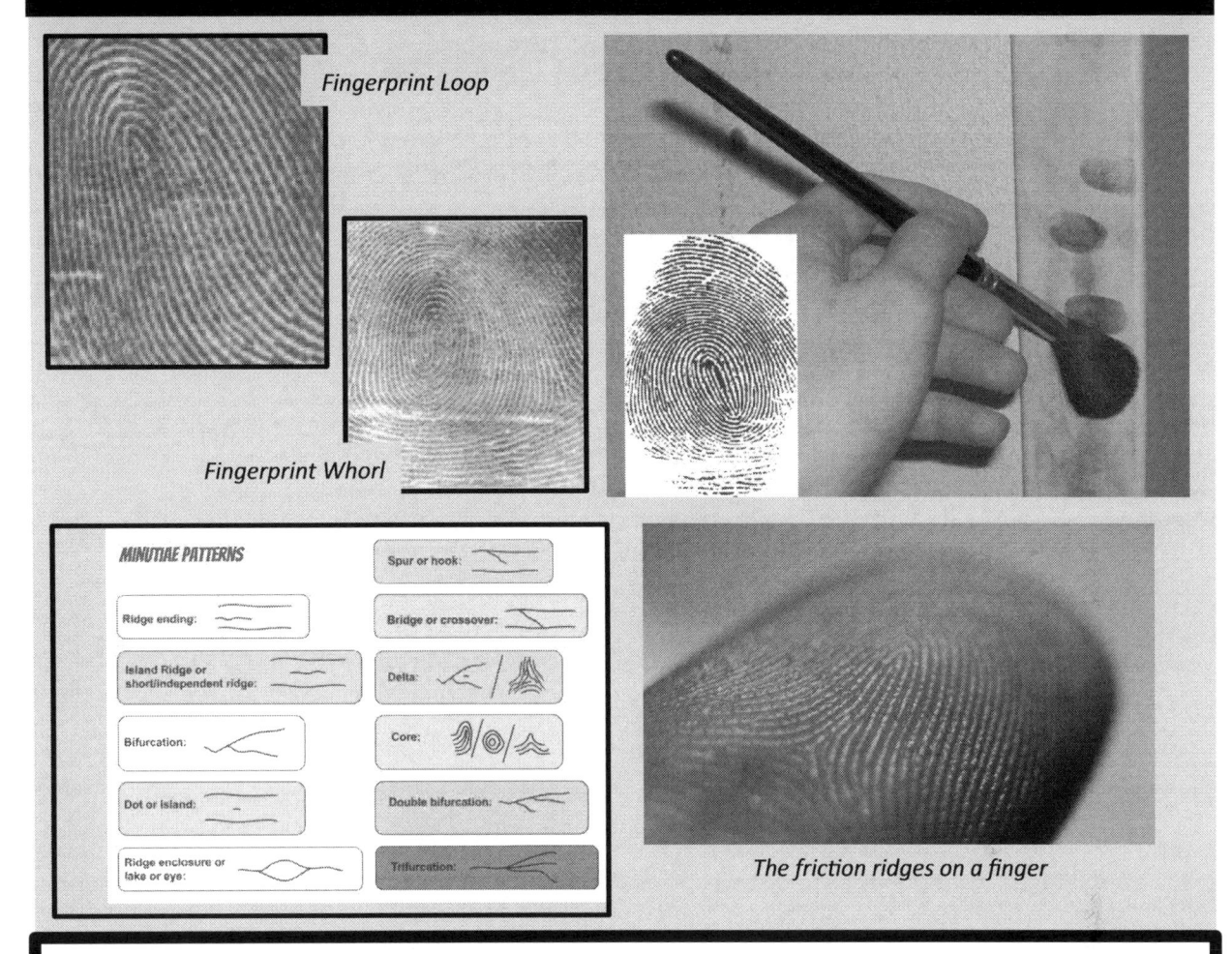

Fingerprint Loop

Fingerprint Whorl

The friction ridges on a finger

Swedish scientists have established that fingerprints left on paper may remain invisible for many years but later be developed, becoming visible to the naked eye. To test this discovery, a fingerprint was developed from a French language textbook which had remained unused in a store cupboard for 12 years, and this was compared with a fingerprint newly taken from the same person who had used book when he was a student.

The Chinese were the first civilisation to record that fingerprints were unique to each individual, and to use the practice of identifying people by their prints. In 1901 London's Scotland Yard started to use fingerprinting as a means of criminal identification, but it was only useful when prints were left on hard, non-porous surfaces. However, it has been shown that when the fingers are slightly damp with sweat, amino acids in the skin's natural oils leave a print on paper. When this is treated with Ninhydrin the sworls of the fingerprint are dyed a deep and clear purple.

It was already known that when using this chemical for analysis, care was essential in handling the paper in order to avoid contamination by the scientists' own fingerprints. A minor nuisance in research has thus been converted into a new aid to crime detection. To develop the prints, the paper is first sprayed with a solution of Ninhydrin, then heated for a few minutes to begin the development process, then left for a day or two until the greatest clarity has been reached. Apart from the interval of time for the 'curing' process, it is suggested that it will be the most satisfactory method in use for the detection of fingerprints on paper and similar materials.

April 2nd – 8th 1954

IN THE NEWS

Friday 2 — **"Pests Bill"** Calls have been made in Parliament for the abolition of the use of gin-traps for catching vermin. They are described as instruments of cruelty and "excruciating torture" for animals.

Saturday 3 — **"Lightweights Win"** Oxford won the hundredth Boat Race against the strict probabilities as statistics have shown that a heavier crew is apt to win more often, which gave Cambridge an advantage over Oxford, as they average 5lb heavier per man.

Sunday 4 — **"Recruits for the Home Guard"** Southern Command's recruiting week began within eleven counties with a total male population of nearly three million.

Monday 5 — **"Women's Answers"** A survey has shown that the marriage rate among university graduates is almost as high as for all women and when asked whether they "enjoy, tolerate or dislike domestic occupations", they also displayed little difference.

Tuesday 6 — **"Budget Day"** Mr. Butler read his third budget to the House of Commons and takes pride in having stabilised the country's economy since becoming Chancellor of The Exchequer in 1951.

Wednesday 7 — **"Easter Bonnets"** The Easter Bonnet Fair was held in London. It was opened by the Duchess of Rutland, with the proceeds going to The British Empire Society for the Blind.

Thursday 8 — **"TV Tax"** A proposal is to be made to a Huntingdon Housing Committee, suggesting that Council tenants who own television sets should be charged higher rents.

HERE IN BRITAIN

"Tudor Foundations Discovered"

The foundations of a Tudor palace have been unearthed during an excavation at the Royal Naval College at Greenwich. They suggest that the palace faced the River Thames and is thought to have been Placentia Palace where Henry VII died, and where Henry VIII and his two daughters, Mary Tudor and Elizabeth I were born.

Originally built in the early 15th Century, the Tudors added armouries and a tilt-yard for jousting. The building had a large river frontage of over 500 feet, with piers for the royal barges. The foundations nearly 3ft.thick and 5ft. 6in. deep suggest that buildings were arranged around a 100-foot square courtyard.

AROUND THE WORLD

"Demonstrations in Paris"

Marshal Juin, Commander in Chief of NATO forces in Central Europe, has openly attacked the French government and opposed the proposal for an internationally controlled European Army.

The French premier and the Minister of Defence were physically threatened by a gang of angry nationalists before police broke up the demonstration at the tomb of the Unknown Soldier and made numerous arrests. Several hundred demonstrators massed around the Arc de Triomphe, scattering pamphlets and throwing stones. Marshal Juin, who spent the day in the country, emphasised that he was not responsible for the demonstrations.

LIFE GUARDS SERVICE

A squadron standard of The Life Guards was laid up in a religious and military ceremony in St. Peter's Church, Hever, in accordance with regimental custom. The Life Guards have a Sovereign's Standard for high state occasions and also squadron standards, but no regimental standard. The disposal of old squadron standards is the prerogative of the commanding officer of the regiment and in former days, when cavalry standards were not always consecrated, they were sometimes preserved in a commanding officer's own house, but after the First World War it was decided that they should rest finally in a church.

This one was given by the present commanding officer to Hever Castle and placed in the 700-year-old village church just outside the castle grounds. Rain was falling when the standard was brought on parade in front of the castle, where the band of The Life Guards waited, the splendour of their scarlet uniforms hidden by dark blue storm-capes. At the end of the service a trumpet sounded the Royal Salute, and to the music of the regimental slow march the standard was borne through the church by a squadron corporal-major, followed by two corporals-of-horse with swords drawn and at the carry.

The Life Guards was formed as three troops of cavalry raised from gentlemen in King Charles II's court-in-exile in the Netherlands between 1658 and 1659 and has become the senior regiment in the British Army, now part of the Household Cavalry. The standards are decorated with elaborate symbols and battle honours, gained through the centuries, and these flags soon took on a mystical quality as it was believed that within their precious threads was woven the spirits of all those that had died fighting in their name. To dishonour the Colours was to dishonour the sacrifice and memory of past heroes.

April 9th – 15th 1954

IN THE NEWS

Friday 9 — **"Tercentenary Celebrations"** Mr. Anthony Eden attended a ceremony at the Swedish Chamber of Commerce headquarters in London to mark the 300th anniversary of the first treaty "of friendship and commerce" between England and Sweden.

Saturday 10 — **"Comets Withdrawn"** The UK certificate of airworthiness of all Comet aircraft has been withdrawn pending detailed investigations into the causes of the recent disasters, including the BOAC airliner which crashed in the Mediterranean last week.

Sunday 11 — **"Honour 'In Absentia'"** Sir Winston Churchill recorded, in London, a speech in acceptance of the honorary degree of Doctor of Laws from the University of the State of New York.

Monday 12 — **"The Navy's New Carriers"** The new aircraft carrier 'Centaur' is to begin her final sea trials this month and her sister ship, the 'Albion', is expected to be in service towards the end of May.

Tuesday 13 — **"US Atomic Scientist Suspended"** Dr. J. Robert Oppenheimer, who was in charge of the construction of the first atomic bomb, has been suspended pending a security review of his Communist sympathies and delaying the development of the bomb.

Wednesday 14 — **"Theatre Blaze"** The Ritz Theatre in Weymouth has been destroyed by fire. By the time firemen arrived, flames were shooting 30ft. into the air and Channel Islands passenger and cargo boats tied up in Weymouth harbour were moved into the bay for safety.

Thursday 15 — **"£1m Zoo"** Plans have been prepared for the rebuilding of the London Zoo in Regent's Park. Moats and deep cuttings would be used so that visitors could view the animals without having to look through bars.

HERE IN BRITAIN

"Blue Plaque"

This year marks the centenary of the Crimean War and plans have been made to commemorate Miss Florence Nightingale's great work in the hospitals of the Crimea. On her eventual return she lived at No 10 South Street from 1865 until her death in 1910 but to date no plaque has been affixed to the building.

There have now been calls for a blue commemorative plaque to be placed on her former home as visitors to London often ask why Miss Nightingale is not included among the celebrated people whose residences are thus distinguished.

AROUND THE WORLD

"Crime Solved"

Six snuffboxes, although in bad condition and deemed to be priceless, stolen last year from a collection which had belonged to Frederick the Great, have been recovered. Their theft from a castle in southern Germany had every sign of daring and precision.

Extensive inquiries led to the arrest of a man who directed the police to a hiding place in a wood where the six boxes were found buried in a lead container. Diamonds which had decorated the boxes had been removed and placed inside the boxes. Some of the gold mounts and decoration are missing and an expert has said restoration will be difficult.

SILVER MAUNDY MONEY

The distribution of Maundy Money, which takes place in Westminster Abbey on the Thursday before Easter, is the modern development of an ancient ceremony said to be derived from when Christ washed his disciples' feet the evening before his crucifixion. In Britain the service goes back many centuries and Elizabeth I personally took part in 1572, in the hall at Greenwich. On that occasion a laundress, the sub-Almoner and the Lord High Almoner washed the feet of the poor people, and the feet then being, apparently, thoroughly clean, were again washed and kissed by the Queen herself. She then distributed broadcloth for the making of clothes and fish, bread and wine. Royalty continued to take part but the last time the foot-washing ritual took place was in 1685. Several changes have taken place since then. Clothing was substituted for broadcloth for the women but that was stopped in 1724 and money was given in lieu. In 1837 William IV agreed to give the pensioners thirty shillings in lieu of all provisions.

This year, in the absence of the Queen, the Royal Maundy was distributed by the Lord High Almoner, the Bishop of St Albans in the presence of Princess Marie Louise. In addition to banknotes and cash (including a crown piece) which have now taken the place of all other forms of gift, the pensioners receive some of the world's most interesting coins presented in a small leather purse, with as many pence as the monarch has years of age – 28 this year and the recipients themselves also number as many men and as many women as the monarch has years. In the days before base metal money, the amount was made up from silver pennies, twopences, threepences and fourpences and are still, today, struck in silver and polished like proof coins.

April 16th – 22nd 1954

IN THE NEWS

Friday 16   **"Meat Prices"** Guaranteed minimum prices for lamb, mutton and beef, were agreed between Australia and Britain in preparation for de-rationing of meat on July 4th, 1954.

Saturday 17   **"Heavy Easter Traffic"** The AA reported that cars were leaving London at a rate of 21,000 per hour as people made an early getaway for the weekend. The weather was bright, mild and sunny.

Sunday 18   **"Ready Made Houses"** Permanent prefabricated houses of many different designs are now available on the home market for the first time. Until softwood licensing was ended these were for export only and the Minister of Works predicted oversea sales would exceed the sale of cars before the end of the century.

Monday 19   **"London Parade"** Large crowds were attracted to the 40th annual Easter Monday London "Van Horse Parade" in Regent's Park. The parade continues, "to encourage a spirit of kindliness to horses and ponies, and to foster an intelligent interest in their well being by those in charge of them."

Tuesday 20   **"Quick Dry"** An experiment was carried out whereby a jet aircraft engine was used to dry out a cricket-pitch and did the job much quicker than Mother Nature. The results are important as the unreliability of our climate constantly menaces our national game.

Wednesday 21   **"TV Equality"** Amendments tabled to the Television Bill in the House of Commons includes a new schedule to ensure that major public events, ceremonies and sporting fixtures have widespread availability across all the main television and radio networks.

Thursday 22   **"New Model Industries"** The traditional heavy industries of steel and tinplate production, and anthracite mining in South Wales are being restructured to increase productivity.

HERE IN BRITAIN
"Myxomatosis"

Seventeen new outbreaks of the rabbit disease myxomatosis have been reported in southern England. Spread by mosquitoes and other biting insects, the disease will increase as the weather gets warmer.
Rabbit-proof fencing and an extermination programme will be adopted as a preventative measure in and around affected areas. The domestic rabbit industry may be affected, with a vaccine being made available at reasonable cost to rabbit keepers. An income of £15m a year is generated by the rabbit meat, fur, felt, and hat trades.

AROUND THE WORLD
"Palazzo Pitti Under Threat"

White ants have penetrated through cellars and drains into Florence's Carthusian monastery and destroyed stairs, seats, and lecterns of the chapter house. More ants have been found in the immediate vicinity of the impressive Palazzo Pitti, built by Brunelleschi, the creator of the great dome of the cathedral of Florence, early in the fifteenth century. Built like a fortress with a basement storey containing ill-lit guard rooms composed of heavily rusticated masonry, the elegant upper floors contain one of the greatest collections of Italian paintings in the world.

PIT PONIES WELFARE

Originally horses were used in the mining industry, above ground, to pull the winch to raise the cages bringing the men back up at the end of their shift or hauling coal wagons around the locality delivering coal. Now, pit ponies, or mining horses as they are sometimes known, are stabled down in the mine and only turned out once a year above ground to enjoy a well-earned respite of fresh air and lush grass. Until recently, under the existing regulations, ponies could be worked for two 8-hour shifts in every 24 hours, with an 8-hour rest between shifts.

New clauses in the Mines and Quarries Act, stipulate that there must be two thorough veterinary examinations per year outside of their working hours and intervals for rest and meals. Animals which work in the dark, below ground, should carry an electric lamp on their collars or bridles and wear a skull pad to prevent injury from falling rocks and debris. The hoof boots must be inspected daily and replaced where necessary. These are made of leather, studded on the bottom with brass or copper nails which will not cause sparks, as iron does, but still ensure the pony can walk with greater safety and sure-footedness underground.

The only exception to the 8-hour working rule would be for the purpose of saving life in an accident. All working ponies must be over 14 hands or 4'6" high. They have the build of a miniature carthorse, and even in the more mechanised pits, the pit pony has an important role and does the jobs that machines cannot do and go where it would be too expensive to take machines. *"He is self-propelled, simple to manage, turns in his own length, and with regular, love and care hardly ever breaks down or needs an overhaul."*

APRIL 23RD - 29TH 1954

IN THE NEWS

Friday 23   **"Antiquities Destroyed"** Part of the Stonehenge complex of ancient barrows, or burial mounds, have been ploughed up by local landowners, despite being registered as part of the National Monument.

Saturday 24   **"Battle Honours"** Next month sees the start of the awarding of battle honours won during the last war. The Battle Honours Committee will focus on Royal Armoured Corps and Infantry Regiments of the Army.

Sunday 25   **"Anzac Day"** Commemoration of the thirty-ninth anniversary of the Gallipoli landings, was observed in London by the laying of wreaths at the Cenotaph and by a parade of Australian and New Zealand ex-service personnel on Horse Guards Parade.

Monday 26   **"Unequal Pay Still"** 200,000 women engineering workers received only 5s 8d (28p) a week increase in wages. Their unions had asked that the women's rate should equal the male labourer's rate, which would have meant an increase of £1 13s. 4d (£1.66).

Tuesday 27   **"Polio Jabs for American Children"** The National Foundation for Infantile Paralysis has approved a start on a test programme to inoculate children against poliomyelitis. The vaccine was produced in the laboratory of Dr. Salk at Pittsburgh University.

Wednesday 28 **"New Move in Icelandic Fish Dispute"** Icelandic trawling companies are to make another effort to break the embargo on the landing and sale of their fish in Britain.

Thursday 29   **"Great Result"** A significant order for steel pipe has been awarded to a British manufacturer, to supply over 350 miles pipe for a gas transmission line in Pakistan.

HERE IN BRITAIN
"New Cathedral"

Despite strong local council opposition, the Minister of Works, has decided to grant a licence for the rebuilding of Coventry Cathedral as he could see no shortage of the materials required for the work.

The council told the minister that their current programme prioritises social building such as schools, housing and community centres, and therefore they would *"probably adopt a spirit of non-cooperation"* and might not accept invitations to attend functions in connection with the cathedral. They argued strongly that the labour required to prepare the site and erect the cathedral would be needed on this other work.

AROUND THE WORLD
"The Petrov Affair"

A couple who worked at the Russian Embassy in Canberra have offered to provide evidence of Soviet espionage in exchange for political asylum. It appears that information was gained from Australian journalists through the Russian TASS News Agency.

Unfortunately, their intentions was leaked, and KGB agents were sent to escort Mrs. Petrov on to a plane at Sydney. However, when it stopped to refuel at Darwin, the Australian authorities intervened, and she was taken into Australian custody for her protection. Press following the story were decoyed by a police car containing a veiled woman, while Mrs. Petrova was driven away.

INUIT ART

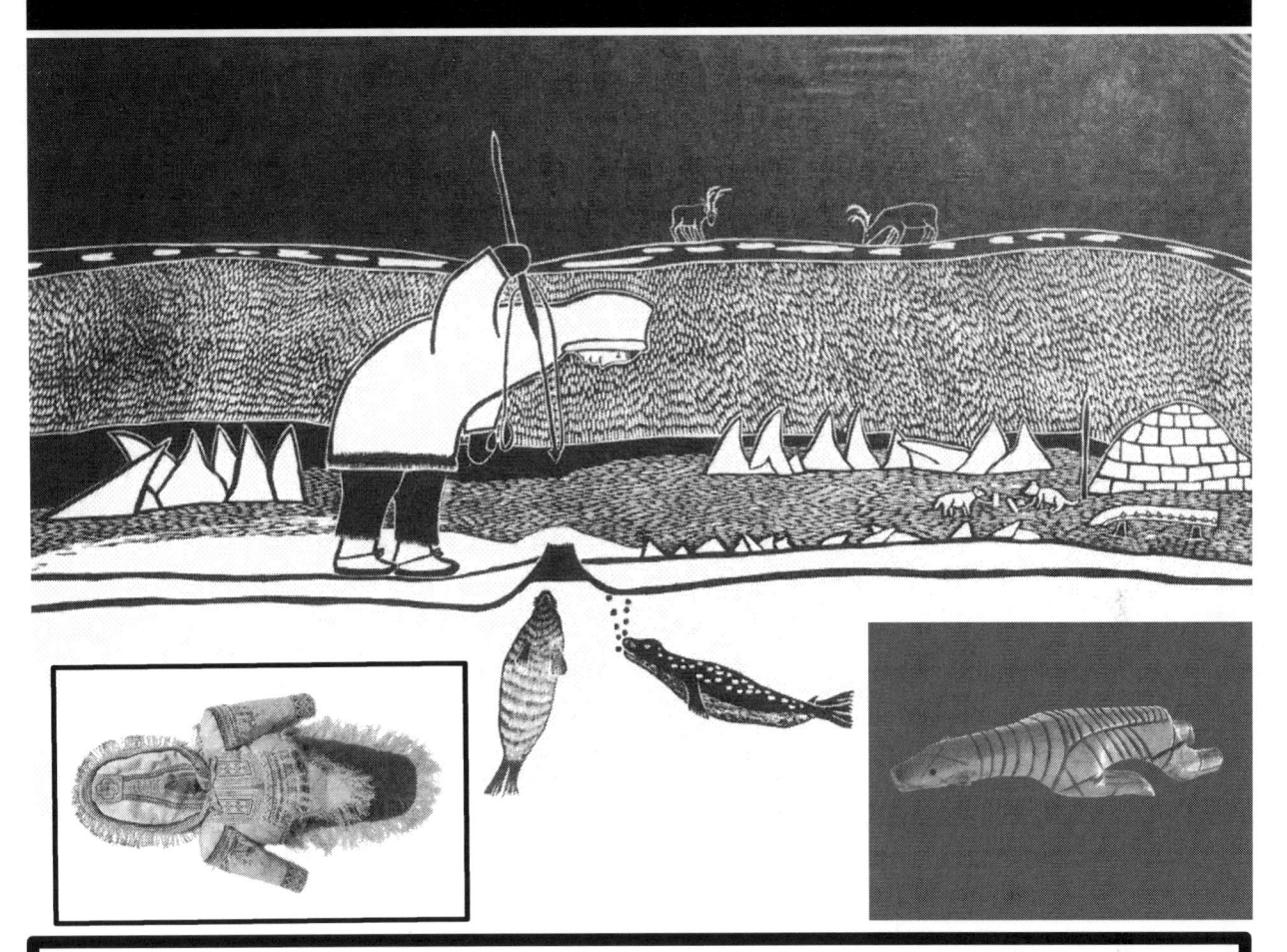

The art of the Inuit people, or Eskimos, is traditionally representational, with subjects drawn from the natural world in which they live, and produced during the long winter months of darkness in their igloos, or during the summers which enjoy 24 hours of daylight. Carvings in stone of polar bears, seals, walrus, birds and fish are skilfully made. These are the result of many hours of observation while watching an animal's every movement to stalk, kill, and then dismember it for food. Much of the work is done by the men, and every boy learns from his father. Some of the simplicity of form is due to the difficulties of carving the stone which varies from soapstone to granite. The hand tools are primitive but effective, and when complete the object is polished with fine stone dust and dipped in seal oil to give it a patina.

The work is quite modern and European in feeling and has a simplicity of form which some have said is redolent of the work of Henry Moore. Their etching on ivory is largely representational - scenes from Eskimo life, such as fishing, children playing, kayaks, igloos. The etching is done with a large needle set into bone and then to create definition, the finished drawing is rubbed in lampblack. The Eskimo women do not carve or etch, but they produce handicrafts and small items of clothing in fur, skin, and feathers.

Much of the work is now being sponsored by the Canadian Government as one means of improving the Eskimo economy which has deteriorated with the declining market for Arctic fox pelts. Although much of the work is simplistic, a few outstanding individuals are now being recognised and shown in exhibitions in Canada, United States and London.

April 30th – May 6th 1954

IN THE NEWS

Friday 30 — **"Addition of Fluorine to Water"** Norwich and its rural area are to take part in a seven-year pilot scheme to study fluorine as a means of controlling dental decay.

Sat May 1 — **"Hilda Welcomed"** The 186th Royal Academy Summer exhibition was opened to the public. Stanley Spencer's controversial figure composition showing his late wife's resurrection received mixed reviews.

Sunday 2 — **"The Red Pasha"** An attempted coup in Egypt by the Cavalry Corps, has been suppressed. A member of the Egyptian royal family known as the "Red Pasha" was among the 50 officers arrested.

Monday 3 — **"Memorial in Malta"** A 50ft. high pillar at Valletta, Malta, was unveiled by the Queen in memory of 2,301 Commonwealth airmen who died during the last war and have no known grave.

Tuesday 4 — **"Celebration Preparations"** Scotland Yard announced that a wide area of Central London will be closed to traffic on the day the Queen returns home from her Commonwealth tour later this month.

Wednesday 5 — **"Art Discovery"** A charcoal study of Christ by Michael Angelo, made on the back of another drawing by the artist, has been discovered during conservation work at the Ashmolean Museum in Oxford.

Thursday 6 — **"Record Breaker"** 25-year-old middle distance runner, Roger Bannister became the first athlete to run a mile in under 4 minutes at the Iffley Road track in Oxford. His record-breaking time was 3 minutes 59.4 seconds.

HERE IN BRITAIN

"London's Trolleybuses"

London Transport have recently announced that most of the 1,800 electric trolleybuses operating in the Greater London area are to be withdrawn and replaced by diesel powered buses. Objectors pointed out that trolleybuses carry 10 per cent more passengers thus operating peak schedules with fewer vehicles, causing less congestion, at less cost. It has been calculated that as diesel vehicles use imported fuel oil, as much as nine million gallons of extra fuel oil a year will be required. Also, the exhaust fumes will only add to air pollution - many remember that the Smog of December 1952 killed 4,000 people in Greater London.

AROUND THE WORLD

"Free Bus Pass"

A Spanish bus company has announced that a child born in one of its buses while the mother, with her husband, was on her way to a maternity home at Tarragona, will be allowed to travel free on the company's vehicles for the rest of his life.

The bus had reached the Ramblas in the centre of Tarragona when the rest of the passengers were asked to get out while the father, an agricultural worker from the village of La Canonja, attended to the birth of the child before the driver of the bus could reach the maternity home.

THE OLDEST RACECOURSE

Chester's "Roodee" is built on reclaimed land, and at 200 years older than Epsom, is the world's oldest continuously used racecourse. The area that the track now covers was originally part of the harbour for the Roman city of Deva which developed on the estuary of the River Dee, and Roman anchor stones can still be seen at the course today. The harbour silted up and fell into disuse following the withdrawal of the Roman Army, and an island formed in the river on which the Christian Saxons erected a stone cross, giving rise to the name "Roodeye" or "Island of the Cross", this name eventually changing to "Roodee". The island gradually merged with the mainland over the centuries, and in 1512 there is the first record of a prize of a painted wooden bowl presented to the winner of a horse race at a Chester Fair.

In Henry VIII's reign the mayor of Chester, Henry Gee, decreed that a race would be held annually, to replace the Shrove Tuesday football match, with a prize of a silver bell being given to *"The horse that ran before all others"*. In recognition of his enthusiasm for the event, Henry's name became synonymous with the sport, which is why even today, horses are known as gee-gees. The event attracted such large crowds each year that in the 19th century a grandstand was built to accommodate the devotees of this sport which had become fashionable to all social classes. In 1903, "Buffalo Bill's Wild West and Congress of Rough Riders" drew huge crowds, but a record-breaking Cup Day crowd of 103,993 attended in 1946 after the end of the war. The Chester Cup has only been cancelled in 3 periods of British history; during the English Civil War, WWI and WWII.

May 7th – 13th 1954

IN THE NEWS

Friday 7 — **"Workers Reprieve"** Dismissal notices served on Belfast employees working on the Comet II aircraft, have been cancelled. All employees will now work 7 hours less losing up to £1 per week.

Saturday 8 — **"Decisive Victory"** The French were defeated by Ho Chi Minh's troops at the Battle of Dien Bien Phu. The Vietminh want independence and an end to French colonial rule.

Sunday 9 — **"Remembrance"** General de Gaulle laid a wreath at the tomb of the unknown soldier. The Arc de Triomphe ceremony last year was the scene of angry protests..

Monday 10 — **"Unemployment Down"** It was announced that unemployment figures are down by 26,300 on last month. The main reason for this was 15,000 more jobs in building and construction trades.

Tuesday 11 — **"Prize Catch"** A 6 ft. sturgeon weighing forty-nine pounds, was landed by a trawler at Grimsby. As by law since the reign of Edward II, they are "Royal Fish", the catch has been offered to the Queen.

Wednesday 12 — **"Synod Votes on The Bomb"** The Church of England Synod will discuss the resolution that *"the existence of the hydrogen bomb is an evil and grievous threat to humanity and civilisation"*.

Thursday 13 — **"Oil Pollution"** An international conference of 40 delegates have unanimously agreed to fix zones in which the dumping of crude or refined oils, in the worlds seas and oceans, will be banned.

HERE IN BRITAIN

"Links With the Dutch"

The strong bond between Britain and the Netherlands dates back to 1550 when Edward VI allowed Protestant refugees to establish their own place of worship in London. Unfortunately, the medieval building was destroyed by German bombs in October 1940.

Reconstruction began in 1950, and Queen Juliana was this week granted the Freedom of the Worshipful Company of Carpenters, an ancient guild with historical ties to the City's Brotherhood of Dutchmen. The Freedom was presented to Queen Juliana in a casket made of oak salvaged from Carpenters' Hall and the Dutch church after their destruction in 1940.

AROUND THE WORLD

"Elephants on The Rampage"

Hundreds of elephants have been invading native settlements in South Africa resulting in devastation among native crops and last week a bull elephant also has gored a hunter to death. Representatives of the Southern Rhodesian and Bechuanaland Governments have been meeting to decide upon what steps can be taken to resolve the problem.

The intention is not to eliminate the elephant herds but to reduce their numbers to manageable proportions. The programme will be long term, designed principally to discipline the animals, removing them completely from the areas where they are a threat to native agriculture.

THE HIGHLAND CROFTERS

The Taylor Commission has spent three years on location in the Scottish Highlands and Islands studying the life of crofters and in particular the problems they face. The conclusion is that it is in the national interest to preserve this agricultural tradition which embodies an independent way of life. It is fair to say that most crofters face a precarious existence at best where years of deforestation and soil erosion have rendered the land poor and marginally unproductive. Most of the landowners have mismanaged and exploited the land for its natural resources, or for the recreational benefits it provides in hunting, shooting and fishing.

Poor infrastructure and the terrible cost of all forms of transport, have led to a downturn in the local economy and depopulation. This has led to a lack of investment which continues the downward spiral and whilst the general standard of housing has been steadily improving, piped water supply and electricity are still wanting in many areas. The crofters' main business is farming and it is estimated that there are about 23,000 smallholdings, most being no bigger than five acres, which support cattle, sheep, goats and poultry. Apart from livestock, eggs and wool are the other major commodities which are marketed.

The commission found many examples of efficient cultivation of crops and good husbandry but much more needs to be done to enable crofters to be more productive. The Commission suggested that better use of pasture would lead to better quality stock, and that if silage production was improved, the need to purchase expensive winter feed would be reduced. In conclusion it was felt that those who fail to recognise the value of crofting would never understand the Highland situation or be able to make helpful proposals for its improvement.

May 14th - 20th 1954

IN THE NEWS

Friday 14 — **"Concern Over Coal"** An increase in disputes has reduced coal production in the first 18 weeks of this year, whilst consumption has increased due to greater demands by electricity undertakings.

Saturday 15 — **"Queen's Return"** Bell ringers throughout the country have been practising their peals of welcome for Her Majesty's return to Britain today from her overseas tour.

Sunday 16 — **"Briton Expelled"** An Assistant Military Attaché in Moscow, was declared persona non grata by the Soviet Government on the suspicion he had engaged in espionage.

Monday 17 — **"Russians in Korea"** A United States Defence summary claims that government officials in North Korea are mainly Soviet citizens by birth and that Russian military advisers have close links to the army.

Tuesday 18 — **"All Quiet on The Irish Front"** The General Election was held in the twenty-six counties of the Irish Republic Polling. The proceedings were broadcast on television and radio for the first time.

Wednesday 19 — **"Strike Stops Trains in the West"** Passenger and freight services in many parts of the western region of British Railways were dislocated by the unofficial strike of drivers and firemen at Paddington, Bristol, and Newton Abbot (Devon) in protest against the introduction of additional lodging turns.

Thursday 20 — **"Zebra Crossings"** Discussing safety first, opinion among local authorities was 120:7 in favour of Belisha beacons flashing at zebra crossings.

HERE IN BRITAIN

"Peers Address to the Queen"

The Marquess of Salisbury in his "Humble Address" said, *"I have found it extremely difficult to find words in any way worthy of assuring her Majesty, on the occasion of her return from her historic Commonwealth tour, of the loyal and affectionate welcome of this House to her Majesty and his Royal Highness the Duke of Edinburgh. How can we tell her Majesty all that she means to us and the whole Commonwealth and Empire? How can we thank her adequately for all she has done to cement and strengthen that great institution by these five months of arduous and even perilous travel?"*

AROUND THE WORLD

"Segregation in USA Schools"

A recently published controversial study looking at continued and widespread segregation of pupils according to race, was conducted by the editor of the Arkansas Gazette.

In 1874, the Senate passed a Bill that aimed to end this practice; however, it was never voted on in the House. The cause was supported by philanthropists from the North, but the funding allocated to African American schools was minimal.

South Carolina, has acknowledged the need for equality in school facilities, but also emphasizing the intent to maintain segregation if the current legal status is changed by law.

MAGNIFICENT STATUE

The excavation of the bombed Mercers' Chapel in Cheapside has yielded a remarkable discovery - a beautifully crafted Early Renaissance figure of Christ. Originally founded by St. Thomas Becket's sister, the chapel had strong ties to the Mercers' Company of London who became its patrons. In 1541, the Mercers' Company acquired the building for their chapel by making a substantial payment. Unfortunately, the chapel was destroyed in the Great Fire of 1666 - and during the more recent war - resulting in the construction of a smaller replacement chapel in 1682. In April this year, as workers were clearing the site, they unearthed a statue of Christ positioned five feet below the chapel's floor. The statue measured 6 feet 5 inches in length and 2 feet 3 inches in width. Although it had incurred some damage, its intrinsic beauty remained intact.

This sculpture, which has generated immense interest, stands as one of the most significant archaeological discoveries in London during this century. Carved from honey-coloured Bath stone, the statue's stylistic features suggest it belongs to the early sixteenth century. It depicts the lifeless body of Christ lying on a rough bier composed of three transverse beams, draped in the robe placed on him by Pilate's soldiers. Traces of colour indicate that the robe was originally painted crimson or purple. The broken crown of thorns rests beneath Christ's head, while his right arm, left hand, and both feet are missing. Evidently, the left arm lay across the body, while the right arm extended straight along the right side. Two wounds are visible, with blood droplets falling from the lower one.

The body is wrapped in a once-white loincloth. Faint remnants of paint suggest that the entire body was once realistically coloured, reminiscent of continental church traditions. The depiction portrays the deceased Christ lying alone, bereft of mourners, shortly after being taken down from the Cross. Although such scenes held no direct dogmatic significance, their purpose was to inspire contemplation and devotion. This newly discovered statue provides a poignant glimpse into the artistic and religious practices of the period, inviting reflection on the sacrifice and suffering of Christ.

May 21st - 27th 1954

IN THE NEWS

Friday 21 — **"Naval Memorial Unveiled"** Princess Margaret, unveiled on Plymouth Hoe, the third and last of the naval memorials to those who died in the Second World War..

Saturday 22 — **"Men Burned in Foundry Accident"** Fourteen men were burned by molten metal in a Sheffield foundry after part of a casting machine, travelling at about 200 revolutions a minute, lifted and caused molten metal to be thrown out.

Sunday 23 — **"Call to Abolish Trams"** After the change from trams to buses in London between 1950 and 1952 there was a reduction of about 30% of accidents involving public service vehicles, but no appreciable change in the number of other accidents.

Monday 24 — **"Balancing Act"** Tightrope walkers Roger and Berthe, made their marriage vows fifty-eight feet above the centre of Toulouse. The priest was perched on the top of the highest fire escape.

Tuesday 25 — **"MPs Vote for a Pay Increase"** A motion, supported by backbenchers on both sides of the House, to raise the salary or allowance from £1,000 a year to £1,500 was won by 280 votes to 166 - a majority of 114.

Wednesday 26 — **"Steam Needed at Atom Plant"** Eight steel towers, each 80ft. high, will provide the link for steam from two nuclear reactors to the turbines at Britain's first atomic power station at Calder Hall, Cumberland.

Thursday 27 — **"Equal Pay"** The Chancellor has announced his intention to make statutory reforms to pay structures in this financial year, meaning that men and women will get equal pay.

HERE IN BRITAIN

"Spiritual Awakening"

Mr. Billy Graham, the American evangelist, ended his London Crusade with an audience of 120,000 in Wembley Stadium. At the close, promptly answering his Mosaic text, *"Who is on the Lord's side?,"* a few thousand men, women, and children poured across the circular cinder track and grouped themselves beneath the evangelist's rostrum to surrender themselves (in the words of his exhortation) *"feet, arms, legs, eyes, heart, mind, and soul."*

Then Mr. Graham invited the multitude still seated to wave handkerchiefs to show that they, too, had made a decision, and the stadium was dotted with flutters of white linen.

AROUND THE WORLD

"Spring Blooms"

The Dutch bulb fields are now nearly at their peak and when viewed from the air, they form a colourful mosaic of flowers. The fields, rich with their scent, symbolise the extensive cultivation and research involved in their production.

The Bulb Research Laboratory in Lisse plays a crucial role in studying and combating diseases and pests that affect bulbous plants and additionally, research has focused on achieving year-round flowering and the laboratory is also working on developing bulb varieties adaptable to various, different, climates.

GREEK GOLD

To the Greeks the gold sovereign is the safest refuge in times of monetary instability and is the accepted tender in property sales and business transactions. Most Greeks will read the daily press reports on the gold market. The Greek Government has now made a step towards restoring the people's confidence in the national currency but the economic climate in the past 10 years has been such that it could not support a healthy currency. An attempt was made after the liberation of Greece in 1944, but the Greeks soon reverted to traditional gold hoarding. The Government is now more confident but is proceeding cautiously for fear of provoking inflation.

The working man kept his savings in gold for many good reasons; there may be no banking facilities in his neighbourhood; by keeping his daughter's dowry in gold coins he protects it from frequent devaluations and it is much easier for him to hide coins than banknotes in his mattress, the traditional hiding-place for savings in the Greek countryside. During the uncertainty of the war, and Nazi occupation, the gold sovereign was the only safe investment asi t could easily be carried away in haste and it retained its value intact in spite of the sharp fluctuations of food prices.

Many Greeks earn a living as gold sovereign dealers. They buy and sell coins of all kinds and give loans against security. The basic gold coin used in southern Greece is the English sovereign, whereas in the north, it is the Napoleon. The traditional Greek lack of respect for the rights of women is reflected in the reluctance of the Greeks to possess sovereigns bearing the effigy of Queen Victoria, preferring "Edwards and Georges". According to the well-accepted rules of the trade one may sell only a single "female" in five coins.

May 28th – June 3rd 1954

IN THE NEWS

Friday 28 — **"Coryton Refinery"** The £15m Welsh refinery was opened by the Queen Mother and will process one million tons of crude oil annually. Deep water berthing allows for round-the-clock unloading of large tankers.

Saturday 29 — **"World's Best"** At Birmingham's Alexander Sports Ground, Diane Leather became the first woman to run a mile in under 5 minutes. She was competing in the Midlands Women's AAA Championship.

Sunday 30 — **"Canonisation of Pius X"** In an impressive ceremony before the main door of St. Peter's, and "for, perhaps, the first time in the history of the Church", the formal canonisation of a Pope was proclaimed yesterday by another Pope.

Monday 31 — **"New Powers to Restrict Smoke"** Local authorities want to establish smokeless zones without recourse to private Parliamentary Bills as existing legislation is not working.

Tuesday June 1 — **"Motto Battle Over"** Wick Town Council, after hearing a letter from the Lord Lyon King of Arms agreeing that *"Wick works weel"* was more correct than *"Wick warks weel"*, voted that it should be accepted as an additional motto for the burgh. It is only one letter different from *"Wick works well"* which the council seemed to prefer.

Wednesday 2 — **"Derby Victory"** 18-year-old jockey, Lester Piggott won the Derby on "Never Say Die", by two lengths. He quietly commented to reporters *"I knew I was going to win."*

Thursday 3 — **"Marriage Bar"** A call for reintroducing "the Marriage Bar", whereby a woman's employment could be terminated once she got married, was overwhelmingly rejected at the Civil Service Conference.

HERE IN BRITAIN
"Wildlife at Chartwell"

The gardens of Chartwell House, home to Sir Winston and Lady Churchill, embody their deep admiration for nature. Abundant with splendid flora, the gardens provide a sanctuary for both local and exotic species.

The Butterfly Border, overflowing with vibrant plant life. has a diverse array of butterflies, attracted to the buddleia bushes and ivy-covered walls.

Their lake is home to black swans, a gift from Australia, while the fish ponds house golden orfe, descendants of exotic fish Churchill acquired from Harrods in the 1930s.

AROUND THE WORLD
"India's Illiteracy Problem"

Almost 81% of India's population is illiterate, and the need for free and compulsory education is vital for the country's progress. Since India attained independence in 1947, less than half of all children attend any school at all in their lives.

Socially the disparity between the sexes means that girls in particular suffer most of all. Many teachers have to supplement low income by doing private coaching in their own time, to the extent that an insignificant clerkship in Government service is both better paid and of greater status.

All Downhill For Big Cheese

Coopers Hill in Gloucestershire is the site for a traditional English event, held at the end of May every Whit Monday. The hill is nearly vertical with a 1 in 2 gradient, is 200 yards long, and it is virtually impossible to run down it without falling over. However, despite the high risk of failure or injury, every year young men will attempt to do just that while chasing a 7–9 pounds wheel of cheese which has been set rolling down the hill at the start of the race. The large round of Double Gloucester is a traditional, full-fat, hard cheese made from the milk of a local breed of cows and has been made in this area since as far back as 1498.

During the second world war, rationing prevented the use of real cheese for the event. From 1941 a wooden "cheese" was rolled down the hill with a small piece of real cheese in the centre and the Ministry of Food had to give special permission for a rationed food to be used in this way. Due to the extreme gradient, the cheese can reach speeds of up to 40 miles per hour and can itself be a cause of injury if it hits anyone in the watching crowd gathered at the bottom of the hill. Each year there are bruises and broken bones and occasionally, fatalities.

The origins of the race are unclear as it probably dates back to pagan times, but theories suggest that it may have formed part of a ritual celebrating the fruits of the land, or in a similar way to the "Turn of the Year" rituals when burning rolls of brushwood were rolled down hills, to mark the ending of winter and the expectation of spring.

June 4th - 10th 1954

IN THE NEWS

Friday 4 — **"Volcano Erupts"** Mount Ngauruhoe on New Zealand's North Island erupted, spewing lava and rocks 500ft in the air. The glow from the lava was visible from 50 miles away.

Saturday 5 — **"Women's Protest"** 40 women, including mothers with perambulators, barricaded a Surrey refuse tip entrance, opposing illegal and objectionable refuse dumping on their local common.

Sunday 6 — **"D Day Memories"** Official representatives of eight allied nations, headed by the President of the French Republic, spent two days commemorating at different points in Normandy, the tenth anniversary of the allied landings in 1944.

Monday 7 — **"East Berlin"** A Communist-organised Youth Rally drew nearly 100,000 young people. On the first day, approximately 5,000 of them took the opportunity to defect to West Berlin.

Tuesday 8 — **"Eight Nation TV"** The first Continental television programmes relayed to Britain and seven other European countries from Switzerland and Rome were received with little interference and the quality of the pictures was generally high. The Rome relay was used to show with clarity and detail some of the treasures of the Vatican City.

Wednesday 9 — **"Haute Couture"** The 7th London Fashion Fortnight began with traditional British tailoring but lacked creativity. Tweed was the dominant fabric, impeccably cut but uninspiring in appearance.

Thursday 10 — **"Rescued"** Four men, including an R.S.P.C.A. inspector, bravely rescued a stranded sheep from a ledge 300 feet above Aber Falls in Wales, they descended using a rope tied to a tree 80 feet above.

HERE IN BRITAIN

"Holiday Getaway"

Fine warm weather for the Whitsun holiday, led to a surge in travellers at London stations with 2,000 additional trains scheduled to accommodate the rush. Stations experienced their busiest period since last summer.

Long queues were observed at Victoria and Waterloo, where over 90,000 people departed on long-distance trains. 40 additional boat trains were put into service for cross-channel travel. Additionally, approximately 2,500 coaches were expected to transport around 80,000 people, mainly to the West of England and the south coast.

AROUND THE WORLD

"Music and Movement"

Haydn's skull has been reunited from Vienna with his bones at Eisenstadt in Lower Austria. The skull was driven about 50 miles, and church bells rang out in beflagged country towns and villages along the way.

The original villains of the story were two of Haydn's friends who were enthusiasts for phrenology and unable to resist the temptation of studying the skull of a genius. They removed it from the graveyard in Vienna where Haydn was buried in 1809 and when found out, they substituted a different skull. It was eventually bequeathed to the Society of the Friends of Music in 1895.

The Queen's Coronation
BIRTHDAY PARADE
★ TROOPING THE COLOUR CEREMONY ★

The Queen's official birthday was marked by the ceremony of Trooping the Colour on Horse Guard's Parade. This year, the Queen's Colour of the 1st Battalion, Coldstream Guards was trooped. Afterwards the Queen, the Duke of Edinburgh, and the royal children watched from the Palace balcony, a fly-past by 27 jet fighters from squadrons of the Royal Auxiliary Air Force. A gun captured from the French at Fort Marabout, near Alexandria, in 1801, was used to fire a 21-round salute at a parade in honour of Her Majesty's birthday at the depot of The Dorset Regiment at Dorchester.

Trooping the Colour is a military parade that involves the seven army regiments that serve the queen grouped under the umbrella of 'The Household Division'. The ceremony is said to be based on an ancient Roman military practice in which the regimental standard was marched in front of soldiers who would then be able to identify it on the battlefield. Regimental flags of the British Army were historically described as 'Colours' because they displayed the uniform colours and insignia worn by the soldiers of different units.

A regiment's colours embody its spirit and service to the home it represents, and before and after each battle, the colour party would 'troop' or march their colours through the ranks so that every soldier could see that the colours were intact. On the battlefield, the flags were used as rallying points and the loss of a colour, or the capture of an enemy colour, were respectively considered the greatest shame, or the greatest glory on a battlefield. For more than 250 years, Trooping the Colour has commemorated the birthday of the sovereign as well as showcasing a display of army drills, music and horsemanship.

June 11th - 17th 1954

IN THE NEWS

Friday 11 — **"RNVR Jubilee Parade"** The Queen reviewed a parade of more than 2,000 officers and ratings of the Royal Naval Volunteer Reserve and its associated reserves from the Commonwealth on Horse Guards Parade to mark the jubilee of the Reserve's formation.

Saturday 12 — **"Aid Secured"** Turkey, the latest country to join NATO, has secured both military and economic aid at a meeting with American leaders in Athens.

Sunday 13 — **"Flooding Throughout The Country"** Heavy rain and storms caused flooding in many districts and affected telephone and electricity services. Several houses were struck by lightning and the rain took a heavy toll of the sporting fixtures.

Monday 14 — **"Renewed IRA Activity"** There was an arms raid on Gough Barracks in Armagh. The IRA raided the barracks seizing 340 rifles, 50 Sten guns, 12 Bren guns and a number of small arms, signalling the renewal of IRA activity.

Tuesday 15 — **"Roman Remains"** During recent excavations in London, part of a Roman temple and cobbler's shop, along with leather shoe soles and an awl, have been uncovered.

Wednesday 16 — **"New Reserves"** The Nature Conservancy announced a new national nature reserve near Bridgewater in Somerset. The land amounts to some 6,000 acres, chiefly of tidal mud-flats, plus a further 300 acres of the channel and banks of the Huntspill river.

Thursday 17 — **"Engaging Design"** According to The Jewellers Association the most popular engagement ring design is a row of three diamonds in a platinum setting.

HERE IN BRITAIN

"Tropical Delights"

The National Aquarist Society's annual show required 1,000 glass tanks, however, a problem arose when some were found not to be watertight. Panicked owners from across the country quickly transferred their fish to vacuum flasks and other containers and fortunately, no fish fatalities occurred.

A team of 25 men worked throughout the night to fix the tanks and despite pools of water still on the floor, judging commenced the next morning. Some foreign and tropical species were new to Great Britain, such as the 'Puffer fish' that inflates itself when threatened and the 'Archer fish' that shoots water to catch flies.

AROUND THE WORLD

"The Abominable Snowman"

Climbers from New Zealand with six Sherpas recently embarked on an expedition in Nepal. Their progress was hindered by dense cover of snow-covered rhododendrons and magnolias, making the path obscure and challenging.

However, while approaching their camp near the summit of a 19,600-foot peak, they stumbled upon footprints which the Sherpas identified as those of the Yeti. The prints, only a day old, belonged to a large creature accompanied by a smaller one. The creature's footprints measured 8 inches in length and 4 inches in width, with distinct claw marks and a rounded impression resembling a thumb.

Taunton Castle

The Museum of Somerset, located within the historic Taunton Castle, has undergone a comprehensive reorganisation over the past 18 months and is now approaching the final stages of completion. This ambitious project has involved extensive structural renovations to restore it to its former glory. Dating back to the 12th century, Taunton Castle was at the heart of a great Somerset estate owned by the bishops of Winchester. Lands belonging to the bishops were scattered over seven English counties and reached to the banks of the Thames at Southwark, but Taunton was their largest estate, occupying thousands of acres in the Vale of Taunton Deane. The Castle entertained royal guests including King John and his son Henry III and in 1497, Perkin Warbeck, the failed pretender to the throne of Henry VII, was brought before the Tudor king as his prisoner.

The Castle was severely damaged during three bitter sieges during the Civil War and in September 1685, it was the terrible setting for the Bloody Assizes which followed the Monmouth Rebellion. Judge Jeffreys, presiding in the Castle's Great Hall, sentenced 144 rebels to be hanged, drawn and quartered. However, the Castle began falling into decay until rescued when in 1874 it was purchased by Somerset Archaeological and Natural History Society who created the Museum.

The primary focus has been the restoration of the Great Hall, which had deteriorated significantly over the years and a spectacular exhibit now graces the floor, a remarkably well-preserved mosaic pavement discovered in the remains of a Roman villa in Somerset. Galleries in the Museum showcase portraits of local dignitaries; an impressive collection of costumes and the local industry of shoemaking. The remaining showcases have been designated for geological exhibits, providing visitors with an opportunity to explore the area's past.

JUNE 18th – 24th 1954

IN THE NEWS

Friday 18 — **"Helicopters Over The Thames"** Scheduled helicopter passenger services from London Airport began to a South Bank site adjoining County Hall because updated flight regulations give helicopters exemption to permit them to operate freely over London.

Saturday 19 — **"Tyneside Dock Opened"** A new dry dock, built to meet the repair needs of the latest big oil tankers, was opened at North Shields by the First Lord of the Admiralty. It has cost more than £1m. and will take vessels up to 38,000 tons dead weight.

Sunday 20 — **"Airliner Down in Sea"** Three British passengers, two women and a 12-year-old boy, lost their lives when a Convair airliner owned by Swissair, of Zurich, was forced down in the sea a mile and a half off Folkestone. Two British women passengers and the Swiss crew of four were rescued after being in the water for over half an hour.

Monday 21 — **"Air Race Winner"** Chief test pilot, Fight Lieutenant Harold Wood, easily won the King's Cup, Britain's premier air race in a Miles Messenger 2A aircraft, which he had borrowed from a Yorkshire farmer. He averaged 133 miles an hour.

Tuesday 22 — **"New Record Mile"** In Finland, J. Landy of Melbourne, broke the world record for the mile and 1500 metres. He covered the mile at in 3min. 58sec. and so beat Bannister's time of 3min. 59.4sec. for the same distance set up at Oxford last month.

Wednesday 23 — **"Remembering the Fallen"** The U.S. military cemetery at Madingley, near Cambridge, will be the permanent resting place in Britain for America's war dead. The cemetery was made over to the War Office in Britain for this purpose by Cambridge University.

Thursday 24 — **"Sir Winston to America"** The Prime Minister and Mr. Eden left London Airport tonight for Washington to ardent cries of *"Best of luck,"* which mingled with the cheers of a small crowd that had gathered to see them off.

HERE IN BRITAIN
"Welfare Foods Distribution"

The Department of Health have announced how welfare foods will be distributed once rationing ends. Currently benefiting four million mothers and children, the service provides reduced-price or free items such as orange juice, cod liver oil, vitamin tablets, and dried or liquid milk.

Starting from the end of June, local health authorities will take over the distribution, using special centres and maternity/child welfare clinics. The Ministry of Pensions will gradually replace food offices and handle the documents.

AROUND THE WORLD
"West German Amnesty"

The purpose of the 2nd Amnesty Bill currently being debated by The German Federal Council, was to "draw a line under a chaotic period" by cancelling convictions for offences which in peacetime may never have been committed. However, while the parties agreed that pilfering of coal or food could be forgiven, views were divided when it came to major black market offences, or tax evasions involving substantial sums. Hundreds of thousands of offenders are expected to benefit from the amnesty; most for petty crimes.

The Thames Barge Race

Thames Sailing Barge Match
Originated in 1863
www.thamesmatch.co.uk

Giralda winner of the 1904 Match

The Thames Barge sailing race was held this month. The idea of the first race was entirely due to Henry Dodd, a refuse contractor immortalised by Dickens as "Noddy" Boffin, the Golden Dustman, in "Our Mutual Friend". A self-made man in the true Victorian tradition, he was born in 1801 starting life as a plough boy. In his early twenties he began organising the rubbish collections of London working as a 'scavenger' sorting 'rough stuff' as it was known. He discovered that he could make more money moving it, rather than sorting it, so from horse-drawn carts he expanded into Spritsail Sailing Barges to deliver the refuse to works on the shores of the Thames Estuary.

The first race, organized under the auspices of the Prince of Wales Yacht Club, (the name is that of the pub where the members met!) took place in August 1863. Eight barges took part including Dodd's own, the WHD, who triumphed and was first home. Dodd died in 1881 and left funds from his considerable estate, £100,000, to sustain the Match. He also left £5,000 to the Fishmongers Company, the interest to support poor bargemen.

This annual Match takes place on the lower River Thames and is now the longest running national racing event for traditional sail in the world. The race starts about four miles downriver from Gravesend and runs down-river past Southend-on-Sea before returning - a total distance of 43 nautical miles. If wind conditions are judged to be unsuitable for getting the barges back to Gravesend for the normal finish time the distance can be shortened. The finish line is usually by the Three Daws public house and spectators gather along the Gravesend waterfront or at The World's End public house on the opposite side of the river to watch the finish.

June 25th – July 1st 1954

IN THE NEWS

Friday 25 — **"Sold"** Metropolitan Railway Country Estates who purchased a large estate and a village in Buckinghamshire say that a considerable area of green belt will have to be developed.

Saturday 26 — **"High Price"** An Italian violin dated 1753 made by the son of a pupil of Stradivarius, was purchased at Christie's Auction house this week for £1,400 guineas.

Sunday 27 — **"Hopes Dashed"** Two pairs of rare avocets nested on a marsh in Suffolk but left after their eggs were stolen by children and an egg collector. The only existing colony is 20 miles south, in a protected area.

Monday 28 — **"Pharaoh's Tomb Empty"** The Department of Antiquities of the Egyptian Government announced that the sarcophagus in the burial chamber under the unfinished pyramid at Sakkara has been opened, and has been found, to be empty. It was hoped that inside the sarcophagus would be the mummy of the king who died nearly 5,000 years ago.

Tuesday 29 — **"State Visit"** The King and Queen of Sweden acknowledged the crowd yesterday as they drove with the Queen to Buckingham Palace. The royal party arrived at Greenwich for a four-day state visit.

Wednesday 30 — **"Eclipse"** The first solar eclipse since 1927 occurred today. Across Britain thousands of skywatchers, using smoked glass or overexposed film, saw 75% of the sun obscured.

Thursday 1 — **"Piltdown Finds All 'Planted'"** It has been determined that the finds made at Piltdown in Sussex, about 40 years ago, were even more fraudulent than was believed last November. The scientific evidence is that the remains are of no great age.

HERE IN BRITAIN

"Appeal For Housewives"

It was reported this week that housewives are the most neglected class in the rehabilitation and convalescence schemes of the National Health Service. Married women need a plan for convalescence as much as men returning to the pits after accident or illness.

When a housewife leaves hospital after a major operation, she is not fit to return to running a home, but there is nowhere she can easily be sent for the kind of care and attention she needs to restore her to full health. A lack of accommodation and administrative clarity enables local authorities and the regional boards to shirk this issue.

AROUND THE WORLD

"Fastest Man on Earth"

Lieutenant-Colonel John P. Stapp, of the USAF, became the fastest man on earth when he rode a rocket-propelled sledge at a speed of 421 miles an hour at Alamogordo, New Mexico, during tests to determine the effect on pilots of baling out at very high altitudes and supersonic speeds.

Colonel Stapp's body underwent a pressure of 22 times the force of gravity and assumed the weight of 3,960lb. The only other man to travel faster than 400 miles an hour was the late John Cobb, who drove his racing car at 403.135 miles an hour at Utah on September 16, 1947.

ANYONE FOR TENNIS?

American Maureen "Little Mo" Connolly won the 1954 Ladies Singles.

THE LONGEST MATCH
WAS PLAYED ON NO. 18 COURT
22ND - 24TH JUNE 2010
JOHN ISNER (USA) BEAT NICOLAS MAHUT (FRA)
6-4 3-6 6-7(7-9) 7-6(7-3) 70-68
MATCH DURATION 11 HOURS 5 MINUTES

The lawn tennis championships began this week at Wimbledon. The first Championships were organised by the All England Croquet and Lawn Tennis Club in 1877 and was for men only. Twenty-two players entered, providing their own racquets and shoes whilst the club's gardener provided the tennis balls with their hand-sewn flannel outer casings. As lawn tennis was a popular sport, interest in the championships grew, and by 1884, when women were finally allowed to compete, regularly drew crowds numbering 3,000. By 1900, doubles and mixed doubles matches were also a regular part of the programme, as were players from overseas, but Britain dominated the winners until 1905 when an American claimed the Women's Singles title.

Although not classed as a regular Olympic sport, it did feature in 1908 when London hosted the games and the first televised Wimbledon broadcast was made in June 1937 with the programme limited to 30 minutes. During the first world war, the championships were held as usual, but many players didn't compete either because they took active roles in combat or were prisoners of war. Two German players, being members of Kaiser Wilhelm's personal staff, were held in British prison camps for the duration of the war. However, during WW2, for six years from 1940, no tennis was played at Wimbledon. In October 1940 a bomb hit the Centre Court causing extensive damage to the stands, meaning when the Championship re-opened in 1946, fewer spectators could be accommodated.

On the opening day the first rounds of singles matches are held, deciding who will continue to future rounds until the exciting days of the finals. Favourites for this year were Czech, Jaroslav Drobny, 19-year-old American Maureen "Little Mo" Connolly, and Australian Ken 'Muscles' Rosewall. Wimbledon is the most sought-after title in tennis because it's "the granddaddy of them all."

July 2nd – 8th 1954

IN THE NEWS

Friday 2 — **"Sir Winston Coming Home"** The Prime Minister has boarded The Queen Elizabeth in New York. The British Ambassador said the US and Britain *"are in full agreement as to how we are going to proceed in the troubled world situation"*.

Saturday 3 — **"Fuel Oil Pollution"** Following a recent conference, the United Nations Economic and Social Council has adopted a resolution to tackle the pollution of sea water by fuel oil.

Sunday 4 — **"Children's Road Safety Campaign"** A campaign of three months, in place of the annual national road safety week, to reduce the high accident rate of children was opened by the Minister of Transport.

Monday 5 — **"Manx Parliament"** Thousands watched the historic open-air parliament at St. John's, Isle of Man, when twenty-three new laws were made official in both the English and Manx languages.

Tuesday 6 — **"Fictitious Advice"** Doctors have expressed anxiety about the dangers of medical and pharmaceutical advertising in commercial television programmes and the danger of 'fictitious doctors giving fictitious advice.'

Wednesday 7 — **"Russians Beat Our MPs"** Two Russian chess masters played 20 M.P.s in the House of Lords. Thirty other M.P.s watched. The Russians were playing together, making alternate moves in the 20 games. After two hours, 17 of the M.P.s had been beaten, one went on to win his game and two drew their games.

Thursday 8 — **"Smash Hit"** Norman Wisdom's first film, 'Trouble in Store' has shattered cinema attendance records created by stars such as Charlie Chaplin.

HERE IN BRITAIN

"Brighton Aquarium"

When it opened in 1872 Brighton Aquarium was one of the two great aquaria and marine research stations in the world. Breeding programmes for sea lions, porpoise and octopus were ground breaking, and it was a model for modern marine research, attracting many eminent marine biologists.

But today it is a shadow of its former self; the 110,000-gallon tank has been destroyed, and of 42 sea water display tanks only six contain aquatic displays, while the remaining 24 have been converted to house apes and parrots.

AROUND THE WORLD

"Gurkha Depot In Nepal"

In a historic move, the Gurkhas, recruited by the British Army since 1814, are set to establish their first-ever depot in Nepal. A suitable location has been identified in the foothills, and the recruitment of these soldiers, who are engaged in combating Communist terrorism in Malaya, will be shielded from Indian Communist interference.

"Better to die than be a coward" is the motto of these world-famous Nepalese soldiers who still carry into battle their traditional weapon - an 18-inch-long curved knife known as the kukri.

RATIONING ENDS

IT'S GOOD-BYE TO ALL THAT
After 14 Years of Rationing

HOUSEWIVES can tear up their ration books at midnight to-night, the hour at which the Ministry of Food relinquishes its jurisdiction over the price and distribution of meat and bacon—the last items on a once impressive list of controlled commodities.

From to-morrow, ration books—everyman's key to the nation's cupboards for over 14 years—will possess only historical interest, except for children entitled to cheap milk.

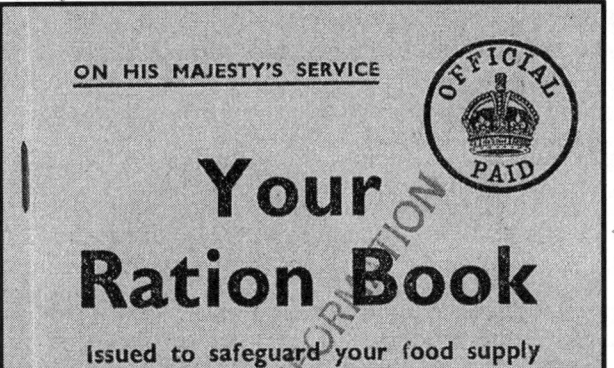

At midnight on 3 July, it was 'Victory Day' for housewives as the rationing restrictions which came into being in January 1940 finally ended. Only the books of children entitled to cheap milk need now be retained until new documents come into use on October 30. Members of the London Housewives Association held a ceremony in Trafalgar Square to commemorate the occasion, while the Governor of the BBC ceremonially burned a large replica of a ration book. Done away with are the coupons, counterfoils, ration periods, registrations, and all the paraphernalia of Food Office rule. The new Conservative Government announced that "*scarcity has been replaced by abundance, austerity by variety, restriction by choice, and frustration by freedom*".

Rationing began in the UK on 8 January 1940 with limits on butter, bacon and sugar. Wartime efforts – including the North Sea blockade – made it difficult to ensure the availability of certain everyday provisions. Petrol had been rationed since 1939, and butter and bacon were soon followed by meat, tea, eggs, sweets and more. By the end of the war, most common foodstuffs were limited as well as clothing, cigarettes and other necessities. Ration books were issued to all citizens based on age and status - pregnant mothers, for instance, were often granted higher rations. Citizens were encouraged to do their part on the 'Kitchen Front' and grow their own food; price gauging and unlawful rationing were subject to heavy fines. Nevertheless, people quickly tired of shortages. Rationing continued post-war as industrial action and rebuilding efforts in Europe often disrupted the food supply and has been slowly phased out with meat the last product to become freely available.

July 9th - 15th 1954

IN THE NEWS

Friday 9 — **"Tax Free Pay Rise"** An average increase of £5 a week extra on MP's present annual salary of £1,000 has been agreed upon. The increase is tax free as it will be paid as expenses.

Saturday 10 — **"Insecticides"** A conference in London is focussing on the use of powerful insecticides in farming. By killing beneficial as well as harmful insects, strains of pests resistant to these new poisons may appear.

Sunday 11 — **"Workers Wages"** A wage agreement in the textile industry in Lancashire will give an extra 9s (45p) a week to mechanics, making their wage up to £442 per annum before tax.

Monday 12 — **"Diplomat Murdered"** A Commonwealth diplomat from the Caribbean Island of Dominica was shot through the head at the weekend and died later at a London hospital.

Tuesday 13 — **"Meat Prices Still High"** A week after rationing ended, meat prices are still higher but easing slightly. At the same time, the quality of the meat is generally better, but many are choosing to continue with fish or chicken for dinner.

Wednesday 14 — **"More Freedom for HP"** Restrictions imposed in February 1952 on hire-purchase agreements relating to radios, television sets, gramophones, refrigerators, vacuum cleaners, cars, motor vehicles, motor cycles, pedal cycles, and certain other goods were revoked.

Thursday 15 — **"Delayed Harvest"** The hay crop is late this year in nearly all districts because of the unsettled weather and although the quantity is good, the quality is well below normal.

HERE IN BRITAIN

"Only the Best"

A Judge this week held that the provision of *"the finest linen and down pillows"* for hospitals in England and Scotland was a valid charitable gift. A Grimsby trawler owner, who died in 1942, leaving £278,000, left, in perpetuity, the surplus income of his estate for this purpose.

The opposing Q.C. argued that such articles were not essential and few people setting up home today could afford them. The Judge disagreed, he said that it was rather a border-line case, *"There are some kinds of illness in which the comfort of the bed is the most important thing in the world"*.

AROUND THE WORLD

"World's Largest"

Mr. Onassis, the Greek shipping magnate, re-established his position as owner of the world's biggest oil tanker when the 47,000 ton, 709ft. long vessel, Al-Malik Saud Al Awal, was launched into the Elbe at Hamburg. Princess Ann-Mari von Bismarck, wife of the present head of the Howaldt yard, named the new tanker with a bottle of spring water from the Zam-Zam well, near Mecca.

Since the Koran frowns on alcohol and the tanker is to sail under the green flag of Saudi Arabia, this was brought specially from Arabia for the ceremony. Some 25,000 people went down to the docks to watch the launching.

QUEEN'S BAR

Terence Cuneo's specially commissioned painting of the Queen's Coronation in Westminster Abbey is to be presented to Her Majesty, Queen Elizabeth, when she and her husband, The Duke of Edinburgh, attend a special dinner at Lancaster House. The commission was made by the Lords Lieutenant of Counties of England, Scotland, Wales, and Northern Ireland and this is the first occasion on which the Sovereign has been entertained by the Lords Lieutenant as a body.

The artist was given a special place in the Abbey looking down on the proceedings and from here he made sketches for the picture both during the rehearsals and at the Coronation ceremony itself. The painting shows the scene in which the Duke of Edinburgh is about to mount the steps of the throne to pay homage to his Queen. Subsequently Her Majesty, the Duke of Edinburgh, Queen Elizabeth the Queen Mother, Prince Charles, and other members of the Royal Family, and many others taking part in the ceremony gave the artist separate sittings to enable accurate detailing of the robes and regalia which were worn.

Cuneo, a British artist worked as an illustrator for magazines, books and periodicals after studying at The Slade School of Art. During the war he produced anti-Nazi drawings and cartoons for Foreign Office publications but is most famous for his paintings of engineering subjects, particularly locomotives and the railway. However, his range of work is vast, from landscapes to portraits and his appointment as the official artist for the Coronation is perhaps his most prominent commission. He is valued for his flair in capturing the atmosphere, either joyful or solemn, of major state and private occasions, together with the personality and profile of those attending. Each work shows the meticulous detail and method that is considered a hallmark of his style.

July 16th - 22nd 1954

IN THE NEWS

Friday 16 — **"Strike at Steelworks"** It is feared that if the 11-day old strike at Port Talbot continues, 3,000 men will be idle by the weekend, with awul consequences for car production.

Saturday 17 — **"Filling the Gap"** B.O.A.C have announced that in view of the withdrawal of the Comets from service for a period, they propose to buy additional, American, Stratocruiser and Constellation aircraft.

Sunday 18 — **"More Fruit Gums"** Rowntree & Co. of York, wish to acquire a site for a new £1m factory in Newcastle. The firm state that their expansion at York is limited largely by scarcity of labour. The proposed new factory would employ 800 people.

Monday 19 — **"Poor Forecast"** One of the worst summer gales in recent years, swept southern England at the weekend causing damage to crops, delayed cross-Channel air and steamer services, and spoilt many sporting events.

Tuesday 20 — **"Fire Warning"** Soon after the owner of a cycle shop in Cottingham, Hull, put a notice headed *"Red Hot News"* in the shop window advertising bicycles on sale without the requirement of a deposit, the shop caught fire.

Wednesday 21 — **"Ceasefire"** In Geneva, the major world powers have reached agreement on the terms for a ceasefire in Indo-China, ending nearly eight years of war. The settlement provides for a partition of Viet Nam roughly along the 17th parallel.

Thursday 22 — **"Queens Carry a Million"** Cunard Steam-Ship Company has announced more than a million passengers have been carried since the war by the liners Queen Mary and Queen Elizabeth. This has not been equalled by any other ship in the North Atlantic service.

HERE IN BRITAIN

"Liverpool Jubilee"

Liverpool's Cathedral has been 50 years in the making so far with building work being continually carried out, even during both World Wars.

The Foundation Stone was laid in 1904 at a huge open-air service, and six years later the Lady Chapel was the first part to be completed. Despite serious delays, repairing damage caused by the First World War, the Cathedral was consecrated in 1924 and its first major service was held during the Blitz. This week amid continuing work the Archbishop of York held a day of celebratory services to mark its Jubilee year.

AROUND THE WORLD

"Lucky Draw - Eventually"

Six members of a New York family are to each have a one-sixth share of a £50,000 Irish hospitals sweep-stake prize won on the Grand National in 1953, which the trustees had refused to pay out because the ticket was in the name of a minor.

In Dublin it was ruled that the baker, who bought the ticket and wrote his baby granddaughter's name on it, did not intend her to be the *owner*. Her name was for luck - and the baker also wrote the names of all the family on the back of the ticket.

PRESERVING VENICE

Architects from all over the world are being invited to join in studies now being made by the Venice authorities for a new town plan. Recognising that the preservation of Venice and its unique character is not just a local or even national responsibility, they have decided to open an international competition inviting suggestions for dealing with the problems besetting the city.

Whilst the original core part of Venice is overcrowded, its atmosphere must be preserved, and monuments of artistic or historical value should be restored and kept in good repair, whilst improving the sanitation and general living conditions of the inner quarter with its intricate network of minor waterways. The foundations of nearly all the stately palazzi that line the Grand Canal are in need of repair. Built when the lagoon was used only by gondolas, and similar light craft, the waves raised by motor-boats and vapporetti going up and down the whole day have caused much damage in recent decades.

Whilst the preservation of the classic beauties of Venice is vital, it must be reconciled with the necessities of over 250,000 inhabitants who cannot live on tourism alone and a way must be found to allow the city to expand along the curve of the lagoon. The industrial port of Malghera is to be more than double its present size, and a new international airport will be built at Tessera on the mainland facing Murano. This will also be the site for the power station, water reservoirs that serve Venice, the ferry- boat terminal, the Customs station, and barracks and warehouses which are at present scattered about the city on land that can then be available for new residential quarters. A Bill for ensuring a contribution by the State to the cost of this scheme is now being drafted.

July 23rd – 29th 1954

IN THE NEWS

Friday 23 — **"Taking a Stand"** Tottenham Council have suspended funding for Civil Defence due to concerns over the development of atomic and hydrogen bombs They are awaiting government protection for its residents.

Saturday 24 — **"Speaking Clock"** Accurate to within one-tenth of a second, 'TIM' the speaking clock, used by telephone users, was inaugurated in London 18 years ago today in 1936.

Sunday 25 — **"Daily Boat Service"** As from this weekend, boats will run from Festival Hall Pier, between the Pleasure Gardens in Battersea Park and other places of interest along the banks of the Thames.

Monday 26 — **"Royal Gift"** A platinum regimental brooch studded with seventy-five precious stones was presented yesterday by the Suffolk Regiment to their Colonel in Chief, Princess Margaret.

Tuesday 27 — **"Watch Smuggler"** A Belgian amateur racing driver smuggled 3,735 expensive watches into the country. They were hidden in a concealed compartment under the body of his Lancia car.

Wednesday 28 — **"Nairobi Arrests"** Hooded Mau Mau informers helped the police to make 1,100 arrests recently in Nairobi, including 255 Mau Mau insurgents. 94 terrorists have been killed in the last week.

Thursday 29 — **"Leaving Suez"** Following the Anglo-Egyptian talks it is expected that the agreement will be signed before the end of September, and evacuation of British forces can begin.

HERE IN BRITAIN

"Saving London's Trees"

The Minister of Transport has approached contractors to prepare plans and estimates for underground garages in three London squares and has now had meetings with experts regarding safeguarding the trees in those squares. Finsbury Square has only seven trees of mature age on the outer edges of the square, while Grosvenor Square has about 50, but the planting in Cavendish Square is dense and varied.

Safeguarding isn't just a matter of depth however, as the chief need is to ensure that the underground water tables are maintained. Only when detailed information has been obtained can the course of action be decided upon.

AROUND THE WORLD

"Mistaken Identity"

Following the Cathay Pacific Skymaster crash earlier this week, the Prime Minister told parliament that the Chinese Government have now admitted responsibility, and expressed their regret, for what they described as 'entirely accidental'. The plane, carrying 17 passengers from Bangkok to Hong Kong crash-landed in the sea.

The Chinese said that they fired on the plane mistaking it for an aircraft of Chiang Kai-Shek's forces who are still attempting to disturb the recently negotiated peace in Asia. A number of planes answered the distress call and eight survivors were rescued, however the mail intended for HM Forces in Hong Kong has not been recovered.

MASTER OF THE ROLLS

The Doomsday Book

Francis Raymond Evershed was the Master of the Rolls in 1954

In memory of
FRANCIS RAYMOND EVERSHED
First Baron Evershed of Stapenhill P.C.
who lived for 20 years at the Grange, Setch
Master of the Rolls, Bencher of Lincoln's Inn
Chairman of Norfolk Quarter Sessions
Freeman of Burton-on-Trent
Born 8th August 1899
Died 2nd October 1966

England has an unparalleled reputation for keeping detailed records of national and local government activity, some dating as far back as the time of William the Conqueror, and his Domesday Book. The problem now however is the preservation of these records, which is seen as the *"inescapable duty of the Government of a civilised state."* It is no easy matter deciding how, what, and when to destroy information.

The staff of the Public Record Office are extremely skilled in the custody of all that is committed to their charge, but their specialised understanding of the needs of historians is frustrated by the indiscriminate referral of papers which have little or no intrinsic value. Records are measured by the linear feet of shelving required to store them, and they have in their keeping now some 200,000 feet (or 40 miles) of records. The present Record Office is under the nominal authority of the Master of the Rolls, and the arrangements for the preservation of the documents of Government Departments are dictated by a series of archaic and unnecessarily complicated laws passed in the 19th Century. Every department has a "destruction schedule," determined by a convoluted and tedious process of consultations and meetings which take many weeks before any decisions can be made. The committee wisely propose to make a clean sweep of this antiquated system and the legislation on which it depends, and to substitute simpler systems.

The Master of the Rolls position dates from at least 1286 and he was initially a clerk responsible for keeping the 'Rolls' or records of the Court of Chancery. He is now second in seniority in England and Wales only to the Lord Chief Justice. One of the most prominent people to hold the position was Thomas Cromwell, a highly influential figure during the reign of Henry VIII.

July 30th – Aug 5th 1954

IN THE NEWS

Friday 30   **"Seraphim Project"** £14 million extensions to Scunthorpe steel works, consisting of two new blast furnaces and their auxiliary equipment known as the 'Seraphim Project' have been completed.

Saturday 31   **"Prices Rise"** The price of milk will increase by 1d a pint to 7d from tomorrow. The dairy industry has made strong objections about the increases fearing sales will decline.

Sunday Aug 1   **"Quiet Bank Holiday Weekend"** Although the sun shone at intervals and temperatures rose at many resorts, road and rail traffic during the day fell well below the average for a Bank Holiday.

Monday 2   **"Illegal Eavesdropping"** Two men were prosecuted for listening in to police transmissions using amateur radio equipment in London. Eavesdropping on the air is now an offence.

Tuesday 3   **"Ship Ablaze"** A crew of 25 and 4 passengers abandoned ship when a Norwegian cargo vessel caught fire at 3am. yesterday, seven miles off Aldeburgh, on the Suffolk coast.

Wednesday 4   **"Osborne House"** Queen Victoria's private apartments in Osborne House on the Isle of Wight, are to be opened to the public for the first time by the command of the Queen.

Thursday 5   **"Supersonic Flight"** Britain's first fully supersonic fighter plane, the English Electric P 1, took its maiden flight yesterday at Boscombe Down, Wiltshire.

HERE IN BRITAIN

"Eisteddford Villages"

This year the Royal National Eisteddfod of Wales is being held in Ystradgynlais, Breconshire. The village is situated at the top of the Swansea Valley, and several other villages nearby are also acting as hosts to the visitors to the national festival.

Every house has been newly painted, every front garden is a patchwork quilt of flowers, and every hedge has been precisely clipped. People have arrived from all parts of Wales and even a party of 480 Welsh people from America. The set subjects for the two chief poetry prizes this year are 'The Flood Gates' and 'The Beacons.'

AROUND THE WORLD

"Do Not Toot"

The new Paris police prefect has banned the use of motor horns in Paris except when necessary to avoid a serious accident, a ban long advocated to put an end to the infernal din at busy crossings.

The universal practice has been to give a prolonged flourish on the horn when approaching a street intersection and, unless warned by an answering blast, to cross without slackening pace. The first effect of the new measure therefore is likely to be either a great reduction in speed or a sharp increase in the number of accidents, which already average over 1,000 a day.

The Commonwealth Games

A crowd of 25,000 watched the opening ceremonies of the Empire Games at Vancouver's new stadium this week. The Queen's message was read by Earl Alexander and greeted with loyal cheers as he declared the games open. The armed services staged a military tattoo and Parnell, Canada's chief 'miler' and captain of their team, recited the oath with the 800 athletes grouped in front. A Royal Canadian Mounted Police band led the athletes into the stadium; first to march past the New Zealand team, the hosts at the last Games, with Canada bringing up the rear.

The four-minute mile by Bannister assured the success of the Games, and the subsequent new record by Landy has gripped the imagination of the Vancouver people and this year so many competitors have entered for the athletics events that it is necessary to hold an extra day's competition The opening ceremony is based on that for the Olympics, but these Empire Games have a different atmosphere, they are much more of a family affair as the competitors, all with a common language, mingle together, make new friends and greet old ones.

The first British Empire Games took place in Hamilton, Canada, in 1930 and they have taken place every four years since then, on an alternative quadrennial cycle to the Summer Olympic Games, except for 1942 and 1946. The 1930 Games were fairly modest, with 400 competitors from just 11 teams, compared to the 2,883 from 46 nations which had competed in the Amsterdam Olympics two years earlier. There were events in just six disciplines: aquatics, athletics, bowls, boxing, rowing, and wrestling. All of them were open to men, but women could compete only in swimming and diving.
This year, 1954, as the dissolution of the empire is gaining pace, the games have been renamed, the British Empire and Commonwealth Games.

AUG 6TH - 12TH 1954

IN THE NEWS

Friday 6 — **"New Coal Mines"** Two new collieries for Scotland have been announced this week, one in Ayrshire, the other near Edinburgh, with the projects costing over £2 million.

Saturday 7 — **"Decline of Telegrams"** Since it was announced 3 months ago that the charge for an ordinary inland telegram would rise, numbers sent have reduced by 15% and that of Greetings telegrams by 11%.

Sunday 8 — **"Air Campaign to Save Trees"** Two Auster aircraft will be used to spray 2,500 acres of forest in Cannock Chase, with a DDT emulsion, in a campaign to eradicate the pine looper pest moth which defoliates and kills pines. More than 100,000 trees are threatened.

Monday 9 — **"Holiday Makers Alarmed"** Cannon shells apparently fired from Meteor jet aircraft flying over the South Side, Bridlington, damaged two houses and narrowly missed a man working in a field. There an RAF firing range only six miles to the south of the town.

Tuesday 10 — **"Violence in Egypt"** Terrorists threw two hand grenades into a British Army families camp at Port Fuad. One failed to explode; the other damaged a tent, but nobody was hurt.

Wednesday — **"Slow Burner"** Underground shale deposits in Yorkshire, covering 1500 acres, have been burning for 10 months, so tree planting on the area has been delayed indefinitely.

Thursday 12 — **"Greenland Party Home"** A British Expedition party arrived at Pembroke Dock after being in Greenland for two years on scientific exploration. With them were 12 husky dogs which will go into quarantine, and then be used on an expedition to the Falkland Islands.

HERE IN BRITAIN

"A Place of One's Own"

Osborne House, on the Isle of Wight, is to be opened to the public. The estate, of almost 1,000 acres, was bought early in 1845 by Queen Victoria as her private property and she wrote,

"It sounds so snug and nice to have a place of one's own, quiet and retired, and free from all woods and forests and other charming departments who really are the plague of one's life."

Since her death in 1901, the greater part of the house has been used as a Convalescent Home but a private suite of five rooms has been left unaltered and locked behind iron grilles.

AROUND THE WORLD

"Colette"

This week, the Roman Catholic Church refused to hold a Requiem Mass for the famous French novelist Sidonie-Gabrielle Collette, as she had been divorced twice. The English novelist Grahame Greene, through the correspondence columns of Le Figaro, accused the church of lacking Christian charity.

However, the French paid the author the singular honour of granting her a full state funeral, attended by many great names from the literary world. She will be remembered particularly for her novel 'Gigi', which was adapted for the stage in 1951, starring Audrey Hepburn, picked personally for the role by Colette herself.

OBSCENE BOOKS BURNT

Obscene Publications Bill

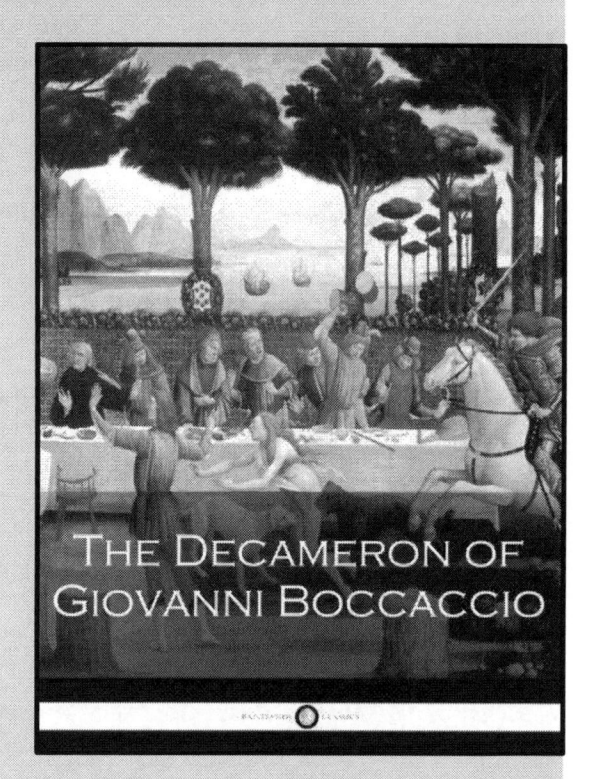

Outdated laws which often have little connection with modern society, are nevertheless still current, and are still applied to the possible detriment of that society. This was a case in point this week when Swindon Magistrates ordered a private bookshop to destroy by burning, 65 out of 348 books seized by police. The Counsel for Defence pointed out that legislation regarding Obscene Publications had been passed in the middle of the 19th century when things were very different. Under that same law, the prosecution was not obliged to say which passages they considered to be obscene, but rather that the onus was on the defendant to give reasons and argument why the other 283 books should not be destroyed. Given the number of books involved in this particular case, it was quite impossible for the defence to deal with each book separately.

Included among the condemned books was a two-volume edition of 'The Decameron of Boccaccio', J. M. Rigg's famous translation with hand-coloured illustrations printed in 1921, which incidentally was also to be found in Swindon Library's Reference collection. The Decameron, being a collection of stories supposedly told by 10 young adults to amuse themselves when they had fled a city to escape the Black Death.

According to English Literature experts it was the inspiration for Chaucer's Canterbury Tales and Counsel for Defence said that The Decameron had been regarded as a classic for 500 years and the police would be held up to the ridicule of the whole country if this book was considered obscene. He further pointed out that regarding the illustrations in this and other books under question *'There is nothing in the wood engravings and nothing in the illustrations which you could not see in any art gallery in the land.'*

AUG 13TH - 19TH 1954

IN THE NEWS

Friday 13 — **"American Flight"** An ex-USAF pilot who 'illegally' flew a small aircraft between the towers of Tower Bridge and under London Bridge yesterday, was to-day on board a Panamanian passenger ship bound for New York. Immediately after landing the aircraft, he took the train for Southampton and boarded the ship *'with all possible speed'*.

Saturday 14 — **"Storm in a Teacup"** India's Prime Minister has said he will not stop Goans from entering Portuguese territories to agitate for their merger with India. *'Goa must be merged with India'* he said.

Sunday 15 — **"Viking Destroyed by Fire"** All 37 passengers and crew escaped when a Viking aircraft was reduced to a mound of foam-covered cinders after a forced landing at Blackbushe airfield, Hampshire. The plane had just taken off and was flying to Nice and Italy.

Monday 16 — **"Traffic Census"** The first traffic census since 1938 started. Over 20,000 enumerators will participate for 7 days. Steam rollers, hand barrows and tanks won't be counted.

Tuesday 17 — **"Plans Stalled"** London County Council have abandoned negotiations with Dorset Council regarding plans to build a new town to accommodate London overspill population.

Wednesday 18 — **"Atomic Waste Opposed"** The Atomic Energy Commission is proposing to dump radioactive atomic waste from Harwell and Aldermaston atomic energy establishments in four disused coal mines in the Forest of Dean against all local wishes.

Thursday 19 — **"Church for Ben Nevis"** The building of a small church half-way up Ben Nevis for the use of climbers is proposed by a vicar in Fort William. It could be a practical expression of the idea of the Universal Church.

HERE IN BRITAIN
"Piper's Lament"

120 villagers from Harefield, Middlesex, headed by a piper playing a specially composed 'Lament of the Lost Glen,' and by drummers from Harefield Boys' Brigade, marched down Whitehall to Downing Street.

There they handed in a letter of protest against a decision of the Ministry of Housing and Local Government to grant permission to a contractor to dump rubbish in old quarries near the village which are known locally as 'The Cheddar Gorge of the Home Counties.' The letter began, *'Dear Sir Winston, With all reverence due to your great office and with affection for your person...'*.

AROUND THE WORLD
"Colder? Bigger?"

New studies on variations in the stature of human beings in different climates have been made by an anthropologist for the Smithsonian Institution. His tabulation of the sizes of the original inhabitants of both North and South America shows the further from the tropics, men and women tend to grow bigger.

In general, he believes that people born in cold climates are taller and heavier than those born in warmer areas, even if the parents were born in hotter climates. Differences in climate could explain the increased size of children and grandchildren of European immigrants to the United States.

Unlucky For Some!

This ship has no deck 13.

XIII DEATH

LA MORT

On Friday, a country thief stole a motorcycle which he rode to the next town where he stole a horse to ride to the next. He then stole a lorry which he drove home and was arrested when he arrived. He should have checked the date! For many, Friday 13th which occurs one to three times per year is regarded as a most unlucky day. Superstitions surrounding the date are thought to originate in the middle-ages and there are dozens of fears, myths and old wives' tales associated with the date all over the world. Some people even suffer from Triskaidekaphobia, the fear or avoidance of the number 13 or 'Paraskevidekatriaphobia', the crippling fear of Friday the 13th.

The number 13 and Friday both have an individual long history of bringing bad luck. In the Bible, Judas, who betrayed Jesus, was the 13th guest to sit down to the Last Supper. In Norse mythology, a dinner party of the gods was ruined by the 13th guest called Loki, 'god of deceit and evil', who caused the world to be plunged into darkness. Peoples of the Mediterranean, regarded 13 with suspicion, not being as perfect as 12, which is divisible in many ways.

As for 'Friday', according to tradition, Adam and Eve were expelled from Eden; Cain murdered Abel; St John the Baptist was beheaded the enactment of the order of Herod for the massacre of the innocents, all took place on a Friday. In Chaucer's Canterbury Tales, written in the 14th Century, he says 'and on a Friday fell all this mischance'. Here in Britain, Friday was once known as 'Hangman's Day' because it was usually when people who had been condemned to death would be hanged and the great crash of 1869, when the price of gold plummeted, was on Friday too.

AUG 20TH - 26TH 1954

IN THE NEWS

Friday 20 — **"Out of Bounds"** Scarborough's Seafront Spa has closed its doors to all Territorial Army personnel below the rank of sergeant, following damage caused by a group of soldiers from a nearby camp.

Saturday 21 — **"Caliph Murdered"** A Muslim religious leader was shot by terrorists in Casablanca. This follows some of the worst rioting earlier this month over Home Rule for Tunisia.

Sunday 22 — **"Win for Britain"** Miss Brenda Fisher, the daughter of a Grimsby trawler skipper, was the third person to wade ashore in this year's international cross-Channel swimming race, the first British competitor and the first woman, to reach the English coast from Gris Nez.

Monday 23 — **"Copycat Designs"** The President of the Board of Trade is to have talks with the Japanese Prime Minister regarding Japanese fashion houses copying British textile designs.

Tuesday 24 — **"New Town in Jeopardy"** The future of Glenrothes, Fife, about 30 miles north of Edinburgh and 30 miles south of Dundee, is now uncertain. It was originally planned as a town where the mining community could integrate with other trades and occupations.

Wednesday 25 — **"Resistance Methods Sought"** The U.S. Secretary of Defence has set up a military committee, which consists of four generals, two of whom were prisoners of the Japanese during the war, to study how prisoners of war can be trained to resist 'brain washing'.

Thursday 26 — **"Falling Crime Rate"** Despite a rise in the number of children aged 8-14, the Home Office reports the number of crimes they commit is at its lowest since 1947.

HERE IN BRITAIN

"Free Dental Treatment"

An inquiry into National Health Service costs, has heard from the British Dental Association that they recommend gradually reducing charges for dental treatment with the ultimate aim that they should be abolished altogether, as they feel many patients are deterred from being treated because of the cost.

They advocate the raising of the maximum age for free treatment from 21 to 25, and abolishing all charges where patients are prepared to undergo preventative treatment to achieve dental fitness.

Without urgent action the association warns that the whole of the dental service will be faced with a crisis.

AROUND THE WORLD

"Missing U.N. Prisoners"

The UN have asked for information about 2,840 prisoners captured during the Korean War who are still unaccounted for. The majority are South Korean, with the rest mainly Americans. In a statement the UN delegate said, *'We are convinced the prisoners are... in your hands and consider they have not been accounted for in a satisfactory manner.'* He demanded information on where they were being held, when they will be released, and details of any who have died or been repatriated. The Communist delegate refused to pick up the list of names claiming it was fabricated and that all persons had been repatriated in accordance with the armistice agreement.

BARTLEMAS DAY

St Bart's Hospital in London (left) and St Bartholomew's Hospital in Sandwich (below) which is the centre of giving Bart's Buns to children on Bartlemas Day.

Saint Bartholomew was supposedly martyred by being flayed alive and this connection has made him the patron saint to butchers and tanners and by extension to bookbinders, for one of their traditional materials for binding books is leather. The Saint is best associated with two institutions, St Bart's Hospital in London and the ancient St Bartholomew's Fair. However, the Cinque Port of Sandwich in Kent also celebrates St Bartholomew's Day each August 24th. Among the most cherished institutions of the town is their St. Bartholomew's Hospital, not a traditional place for the sick, but a tranquil setting for the aged men and women of the town.

The records of the hospital give full details of its foundation in the reign of Richard the Lionheart, who landed at Sandwich on his return from the Crusades. There were four founding knights, and one of them, Sir Henry de Sandwich, has his tomb in the chapel of the hospital. These knights gave their land to provide a home for maimed mariners and the poor and elderly of the city to end their days in peace, and for more than 750 years, the 'brothers and sisters,' chosen by town worthies have lived on this same quiet site.

About 55 years ago the old hospital building of the middle ages was replaced by a quadrangle of little cottages, each standing in its garden with the ancient chapel, with its Norman arches, remaining in the centre. A service is held in the chapel on Bartlemas Day following which, the children of Sandwich run round the chapel and receive a current bun from the trustees of the hospital. The adults who attend the service are presented with a less edible 'St Bart's biscuit', a wafer stamped with the arms of Sandwich and the legend of the foundation.

Aug 27th - Sept 2nd 1954

IN THE NEWS

Friday 27 — **"Shoppers' Grumbles"** The British Standards Institution is to launch a Consumer Advisory Council of 30 people who will investigate dissatisfied customers' complaints.

Saturday 28 — **"Cable Ship Damaged"** The new British cable repair ship, designed to maintain cable networks in Far Eastern waters has collided with a Danish vessel in the Thames.

Sunday 29 — **"Plague Sunday"** in the Derbyshire village of Eyam, a memorial service recalled how the villagers cut themselves off from the world in 1665 to prevent the spread of the bubonic plague.

Monday 30 — **"England Medal"** Roger Bannister achieved victory for England at the European Athletics Championships in Switzerland yesterday by winning the 1500 metres in 3min 43.8 sec.

Tuesday 31 — **"Red Threat"** President Eisenhower has spoken of the readiness of the combined US armed forces to combat the Communist 'insatiable' determination to dominate the world.

Wed Sept 1 — **"Hottest Day"** In southern England and East Anglia many towns had more than 11 hours of sunshine and for the first time this summer there were temperatures of 80deg. (27C) on the East coast.

Thursday 2 — **"Runaway Fire"** A fire brigade in Northern Ireland chased a lorry for six miles before catching it up and extinguishing a fire on board. The driver was totally unaware of the blaze.

HERE IN BRITAIN

"Poor Year for Bees"

It appears that this winter is going to be the worst within living memory for bees. Each hive must go to winter with a minimum of 30lb. of stores if it is to survive until the spring and in most areas, the bees depend on their gatherings from mid-June to the end of July.

Persistent rain and lack of warmth and sunshine during these two months this year are to blame, nectar, the raw material from which honey is made, is only secreted by flowers in reasonably warm weather, and the bees are able to gather it only when it is not raining.

AROUND THE WORLD

"Italy's Land Reform"

Many of Italy's agricultural workers have struggled to make an adequate living off the land for centuries. Some still live in caves or makeshift shelters as their families have for generations.

However, two Land Reform acts passed in 1950 are slowly changing the past and giving them hope for a brighter future. Before, out of 18 million Italian farmers, 500 owned most of the land.

Following the reform, larger pieces of land are confiscated, enabling the average worker now to have 30 acres of land to farm, and a two-storey house for him and his family to live in.

GRASMERE SPORTS

Every August Bank Holiday Sunday, the small Lake District market town of Grasmere welcomes thousands of visitors from all over the North of England to join in the annual show and sports day, which boasts among the usual attractions, some events which are peculiar to Cumberland and Westmorland.

Cumberland wrestling involves the wrestlers standing chest to chest, grasping each other around the body with their chins on their opponent's right shoulder. The aim is to unbalance your opponent or make them lose their grip. If any part of the wrestler's body apart from the feet touches the ground that person has lost the bout. The traditional costume consists of long johns with a pair of satin breeches and an embroidered vest. There is also fell running, from the sports ground, up either Rydall Fell or Butter Fell and back, approximately 1.4 miles over rough terrain and very steep gradient in parts. Both the wrestling and running events are hugely popular with all ages, with classes from Under 9's to Seniors. In the fell running it isn't unusual to see over 70-year-olds competing - and winning!

The third event of note is the Hound Trailing, with dogs racing over fields and fells, following a trail of paraffin and aniseed laid by 'trailers' on the morning of the event. The aim is to confuse the hounds by marking out a deliberately challenging course. The dogs are descendants of fox hounds, especially bred for their speed and stamina, with races for young dogs covering 5 miles, and 10 miles for adult hounds. Completion times are usually within 30 minutes, which is remarkable given the terrain involved. Although these types of sporting events may form part of many local shows in England, none can claim such a long history and unique flavour as that of Grasmere.

SEPT 3RD - 9TH 1954

IN THE NEWS

Friday 3 — **"Storm Damage"** An ancient mulberry tree, which local tradition says was planted in 1628 by the poet Milton, has been felled by a gale in Stowmarket, Suffolk.

Saturday 4 — **"Fair Isle for the Nation"** The National Trust for Scotland announced to-day that they have taken over Fair Isle, Shetland, from its owner, Mr. George Waterston, the Edinburgh ornithologist. Fair Isle was bought by Mr. Waterston in 1948 and since then has been developed as a bird observatory of world-wide reputation.

Sunday 5 — **"Bumper Harvest"** Tomato growers on Guernsey in the Channel Islands have reported that 42,211 tons of tomatoes have been imported into Britain so far this season.

Monday 6 — **"Air Disaster"** a KLM airliner en route from Amsterdam to New York crashed into the River Shannon, killing 28 American passengers. The cause of the accident is unknown.

Tuesday 7 — **"Fossils of Tomorrow"** According to the International Union for the Protection of Nature, many wildlife species have declined in recent years and though climatic changes may be partly responsible, man still poses the biggest threat to the natural world.

Wednesday 8 — **"Influence of Television"** The Nuffield Foundation is to make an in-depth study of the effects of television on viewers, particularly children and young people. The physical, psychological and spiritual influences will be studied.

Thursday 9 — **"Landmark for S. Pacific Area"** The S.E. Asia collective defence treaty was signed in Manilla by the eight nations taking part in the conference. SEATO comprises the U.S., Australia, New Zealand, France, U.K., Philippines, Thailand and Pakistan.

HERE IN BRITAIN

"Record Shark"

About 12 miles south-west of Looe, a blue shark over 8ft. long and weighing 155lb. - a new British record for a rod-caught fish of this kind - was landed by a holidaymaker on his first venture with the shark boats.

He was fishing with harness in quite a rough sea, and felt a bite almost as soon as the last bait of the day, a pilchard, went in. He played the shark for about a quarter of an hour, after which it made a fast dive and a tussle lasting 30 to 45 minutes ensued before the fish was finally hauled aboard.

AROUND THE WORLD

"Water Mark Error"

A watermark error has been found in the production of stamps of recent date for British Guiana, St. Lucia and Basutoland and printed in 1951 and 1952. All colonial stamps are produced to the order of the Crown Agents for oversea governments and are watermarked with an all over device consisting of a crown and the letters CA in script.

The watermark is impressed in the paper during manufacture by a 'dandy roll' to which are affixed some 6,900 Crown CA 'bits'. All these 'bits' are normally identical, but the discovery shows that a completely different shaped crown was introduced in one instance.

FAROE FISHING

Herring have for many years been caught in the Faroe fjords and exported to Denmark, while Faroe ships have netted herrings near Iceland and landed the catch there. Last year for the first time it became apparent that vast shoals of the large, fat, ocean type of herring were to be found in the waters near the Faroes, and a large part of the fishing fleet was immediately diverted. The total for the season was about 140,000 barrels, and practically the entire catch was exported to Russia. This year, up to 160,000 barrels are guaranteed to the Soviet Union and the greater part of the fishing fleet is concentrating on catching these delicious fish and the Faroe fishing industry stands at a turning point in its history.

The Faroes are a small group of 21 islands, with a total population of over 30,000, which lie between Shetland and Iceland in the North Atlantic. To many in Britain they are just a name on the Shipping Forecast, but recent history shows there are strong links with our country. Like Scotland, they were originally part of Norway and inhabited by Vikings but from the beginning of the 19th century, they came under Danish rule.

The islands are dotted with little townships that formerly subsisted by small scale farming and fishing, but the Faroese economy benefited hugely when the British fishing industry invested in steam trawlers at the end of the 19th century and the Faroese fishing industry was born. Up until the second world war, the exports were mostly of salted and 'klip' or air-dried fish, bound for Mediterranean countries but with the advent of war, export to the Continent was discontinued and all their catches of fresh fish were transported to British markets, supplying up to a quarter of all the fish consumed in our country.

SEPT 10ᵀᴴ - 6ᵀᴴ 1954

IN THE NEWS

Friday 10 — **"More for Australia"** The Oversea Migration Board has recommended that the assisted passage scheme to Australia should be renewed. So far, 147,768 men, women and children have benefited.

Saturday 11 — **"Tiger Comic"** The sporting comic was launched and Roy of the Rovers made his first appearance on the cover, recounting the life of Roy Race and his team Melchester Rovers.

Sunday 12 — **"Domesday Book Village"** Damage to a dozen houses in Huncoat, Accrington, a village mentioned in the Domesday Book as having belonged to Edward the Confessor, are believed to be caused by subsidence resulting from mining operations.

Monday 13 — **"Summer School"** The National Coal Board started a summer school at Oxford University for coal miners this week. The participants are to be accommodated in the colleges.

Tuesday 14 — **"Labour Pains"** At the British Pharmaceutical Conference, a leading chemist said, *'I am not prepared yet to say if there is anything in the old wives' tale that raspberry leaf tea can ease the pain of childbirth, but we are proceeding with our research.'*

Wednesday 15 **"Battle of Britain Fly Past"** Five R.A.F. Hunter jets took part in the fly-past over London to commemorate the Battle of Britain. They followed five Swifts and all 10 aircraft flew at 575 miles an hour.

Thursday 16 — **"Price of a Cuppa to Rise"** The price of all blends of tea will be increased by about 8d (3p). a lb. One of the reasons is the increased demand for tea in the U.S., where there has been a campaign to attract Americans back to their old tea-drinking habits.

HERE IN BRITAIN

"Hop Harvest"

Hop picking has begun in Kent. Originally the work was labour intensive, and seasonal workers were needed at harvest time. Whole families, usually from London, would arrive in the country for three weeks in September for picking and many saw it as a kind of holiday, a chance to exchange city grime for fresh air in the countryside.

Living-huts were provided for the workers, with latrines and a wash house. Hot baths could be had for a charge of 2d (1p). However, since the end of the war, more farmers are harvesting mechanically which is proving more reliable and dependable than manual labour.

AROUND THE WORLD

"French Teachers Say NON!"

Teachers in France had parity of conditions and salary with the armed forces and civil servants. However, pay awards since 1948 to these sectors have not been extended to teachers. Last July the French Teachers' Unions threatened strike action if cost of living increases were not forthcoming.

Last Monday saw 45,000 students sitting their first national examinations, but there will be no one to mark the papers, unless the pay demands are met. The teachers have denounced the current token offer as 'derisory' and are standing firm. A union delegation is to meet with the Prime Minister to try and break the deadlock.

TO THE MANOR BORN

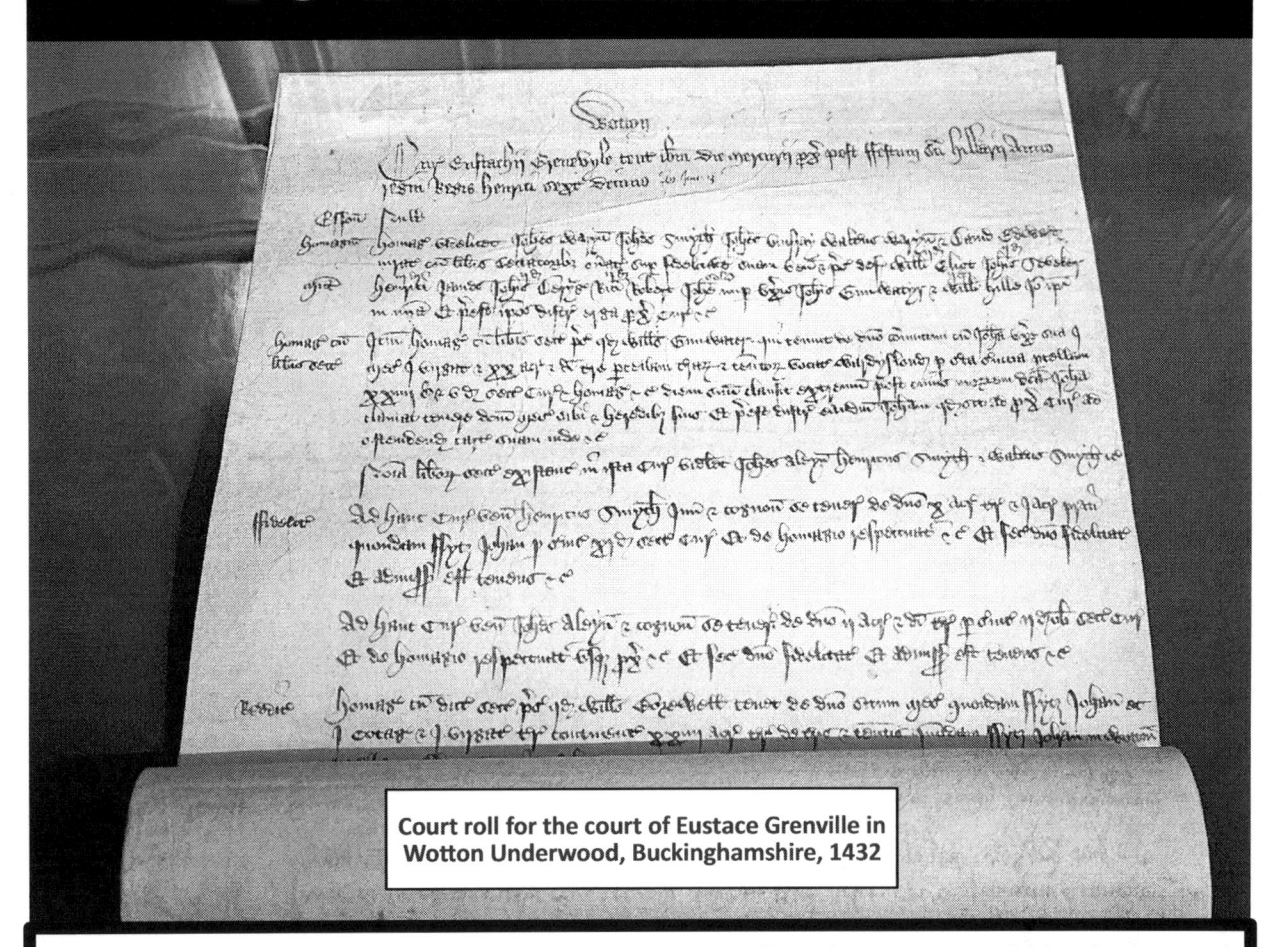

Court roll for the court of Eustace Grenville in Wotton Underwood, Buckinghamshire, 1432

A Lordship was a landed estate which first appeared under William the Conqueror which, when granted, also imposed certain responsibilities such as providing a number of armed men and equipment to fight the Monarch's wars. The Lord had to govern the peasants who worked the land, whether by agriculture, fishing or forestry and to maintain law and order. However, the benefits were significant as he could charge rents, either for land or buildings, raise levies for the use of the village mill or the river for fishing, and charge tolls on bridges.

When it came to administering justice, the Lord decided on the level of fines he would impose and the revenue from a large manor could be substantial. In the 19th century, with the expansion of industry, many land agreements were made, whereby utility companies paid ground rent for pipes that ran under, or access roads that ran over, the Lord's land.

All these agreements were recorded in the Manorial Rolls which are still held in Public Record Offices, the oldest being handwritten on sheepskin or vellum. In the last century, a solicitor practising in Essex, and acting as steward to landowners in Essex, Suffolk and Norfolk, started buying Lordships whenever the opportunity arose and his son continued to add to this portfolio known as 'The Beaumont Collection', which is now being put up for sale.

Twenty seven will be put up for auction, and a further twenty nine for private sale. Some people will be interested in gaining the title Lord of the Manor, which comes with the estate and any grazing, fishing, or forestry rights pertaining to the land. Others may just want to become a part of the unique history of our island. Either way, there is bound to be a great deal of interest in the sale of these Lordships.

SEPT 17TH - 23RD 1954

IN THE NEWS

Friday 17 — **"Fatal Attraction to Children"** The practice by manufacturers of colouring medical tablets was condemned by the British Pharmacopoeia Commission. Their secretary said, *'Not only do the coloured tablets provide a danger to young children; they also provide a potential danger involving faulty identification'*.

Saturday 18 — **"NFU Up in Arms"** In June the Government appealed to farmers to increase the pig population by 1,060,000. Today, bacon factories are refusing to accept thousands bred for bacon since then and now being sold at auction at 'give away' prices. Pig farmers are losing money at an alarming rate.

Sunday 19 — **"Detector Vans"** Nine Post Office vehicles equipped with television detection instruments are to be used to hunt down TV licence dodgers.

Monday 20 — **"Russian Business"** Russia has won a British contract, over America, to supply tractors, mining and steel manufacturing equipment for the diamond mining industry in India.

Tuesday 21 — **"Mortgage Rates Cut"** The Halifax Building Society is to reduce its mortgage rate from 4½% to 4% but has been told by the Bank of England that they must also reduce the rate offered to investors.

Wednesday 22 — **"Big Crowds at Roman Ruins"** Several thousand people queued to see the remains of a Roman temple, columns, an altar and a marble head of the god Mithras, unearthed on a construction site at Walbrook, London. Building was to have started last Monday.

Thursday 23 — **"Migrant Workers"** The 700 Jamaicans so far to immigrate here to look for work, arrived in Southampton this week. They had paid £100 for the one-way ticket to Britain.

HERE IN BRITAIN

"G.P.O. Search for Pirates"

Believing that there are still many people without a TV licence, the Post Office sent out nine cars equipped with special detection instruments. The G.P.O. knows the number of licences taken out and the number of sets sold: the difference suggests that there are between 100,000 and 200,000 unlicenced sets.

Existing licences are marked on a map in each postal district. The Post Office engineers estimate that over a distance of 100ft., which is the normal working range of their instruments, they can pin-point a working receiving set to within 6in.

AROUND THE WORLD

"Tobacco Code"

Due to recent scientific research concerning the effect of cigarette smoking, the U.S. Federal Trade Commission has proposed the adoption of advertising standards in the tobacco industry. Advertisers should not claim directly or by implication that *'cigarette smoking or the smoking of any particular brand of cigarettes'* is *'not harmful or non-irritating'* nor that they *'contain less nicotine, tar or resin'*. They should not refer to the *'throat, larynx, or any other part of the body, nor to digestion, energy, or nerves'* but should limit their advertising to the subjects of *'quality, taste, flavour, and enjoyment'*.

THE PROMENADE CONCERTS

Nothing that the BBC cameras can offer, be it close-ups of the conductor's face, a promenader's balloon or Union Jack, or a trombonist's extended cheeks, can rival the excitement of actually being part of the uninhibited throng of the Last Night of the Proms. But we cannot all be there and television this week broadcast, for the first time, the combination of Sir Henry Wood's 'Fantasia on British Sea Songs', Sir Edward Elgar's setting of 'Land of Hope and Glory', Sir Hubert Parry's setting of William Blake's 'Jerusalem' and 'Rule Britannia!'

There have now been Promenade Concerts – literally, concerts where you can walk about, in London, for more than a hundred years and our present series can reasonably trace its ancestry to the entertainments in the public gardens of Vauxhall, Ranelagh and Marylebone in the eighteenth century. The original English promenade concerts at the Lyceum Theatre in 1838 were conducted by Musard and consisted of instrumental music of a light character, containing overtures, solos for a wind instrument and dance music (quadrilles and waltzes). The change from theatre to concert hall, Queen's Hall, was made by Robert Newman when, in 1895, he started a series with Henry J Wood as conductor. Newman wished to generate a wider audience for concert hall music by offering low ticket prices and an informal atmosphere, where eating, drinking and smoking were allowed. He said, *"I am going to run nightly concerts and train the public by easy stages. Popular at first, gradually raising the standard until I have created a public for classical and modern music."*

After the Queen's Hall was bombed in 1941 the Proms moved to the Albert Hall where their policy remains, classics plus new works and among the established artists, promising newcomers.

Sept 24th - 30th 1954

IN THE NEWS

Friday 24 — **"Two Million Telephones"** The Postmaster-General presented a golden coloured telephone to the Constable of the Tower of London, to commemorate the installation of the 2,000,000th telephone in the London telecommunications region.

Saturday 25 — **"Breakfast Order"** Britain has reached an agreement to purchase 220,000 tons of Danish bacon next year, with the price remaining unchanged from the current contract.

Sunday 26 — **"Flood Go-Ahead"** The Sheffield and Peak District branch of the Council for the Preservation of Rural England has formally supported the proposed flooding of Amber Valley for a reservoir near Chesterfield.

Monday 27 — **"Poles to be Extradited"** The Foreign Office have been notified that Poland will demand the extradition of the seven Polish trawler men who locked up their captain and the political officer and sailed into Whitby harbour to seek political asylum.

Tuesday 28 — **"City May Ban Horror Comics"** Ministers throughout Glasgow have been shocked by the blood curdling story in an American comic book of 'the vampire with iron teeth who strangled and devoured two little boys' which sent hundreds of children, armed with knives and sticks, screaming through a cemetery searching for the monster.

Wednesday 29 — **"Improved Visibility"** The Minster of Transport is investigating a proposal to mandate both off-side and near-side driving mirrors for motor vehicles, instead of the current requirement for one mirror.

Thursday 30 — **"Waitresses Outnumber Guests"** Twenty-two masters were absent from the civic tea party held at the Winter Gardens after Blackpool Grammar School's speech day because their wives had not been invited.

HERE IN BRITAIN

"Former Royal Yacht"

The former Royal Yacht, 'Victoria and Albert' is being prepared for breaking up. Laid down in 1897, she is now in Portsmouth Dockyard and when her mizzen mast was removed a half-sovereign, five-shilling piece and half-crown were found under its footing.

According to official records, a sovereign, five-shilling piece, two-shilling piece, and sixpence, gifts from Queen Victoria, are under the footing of the mainmast, and under the footing of the foremast are a sovereign and a penny, the gifts of King Edward VII when he was Prince of Wales.

AROUND THE WORLD

"Fuel Explosion"

The death toll from the NATO air station disaster in West Germany has reached 31. An underground tank containing jet fuel for fighter planes exploded, which caused 75 gallons of petrol on the ground above the tank, intended for a fire suppression demonstration, to catch fire.

Witnesses described a rumbling sound followed by a 200-foot burst of flame. The explosion severed a pipe connecting the first tank to a second, the fuel to spilt across adjacent fields, and 300,000 gallons of fuel were lost. Initial suspicions of sabotage are unsubstantiated.

WOULD YOU CREDIT IT?

Nobody needs to go short of credit nowadays and rarely do. From household machines and labour-saving devices, such as washing machines and refrigerators, to carpets and furnishings, from radio and television sets to the car or motorcycle for leisure, all can be bought with loans.

Hire-purchase, is an almost indispensable boon to producers of goods and services. One down payment and a pledge to pay instalments bring the farmer his tractor and hen batteries, the haulier his fleet of lorries, the shopkeeper his smart shop fittings, the butcher and grocer their refrigeration safes, and the large manufacturer his railway wagons. Before long, if a few of the finance companies have their way, it will also be possible for the house owner to foot the bill for his building repairs in the same painless way. Furniture retailers say that three-quarters of their whole trade is on hire purchase and so are at least half the home sales of television sets and one new car in ten is bought on an instalment plan.

Back in the 1930's the middle-classes could manage to save up to buy the half-luxuries and conveniences that they wanted, and hire purchase was a working-class device for obtaining, not luxuries, but necessaries such as furniture. At that time hire purchase was a class symbol, but nowadays, the middle-class have little opportunity to save for the multitude of expensive gadgets that make their life easier or more agreeable.

But hire purchase is still not the full story of credit in Britain. There are a host of tallymen who are busy in working-class districts pushing high interest rate loans and some stores offer 'budget credit accounts' for customers who have a bank account on which a monthly banker's order may be drawn.

OCT 1ST – 7TH 1954

IN THE NEWS

Friday 1 — **"NHS heading for Trouble"** The Labour party warned that thousands of skilled and experienced staff had left the service in the past few years because they could not afford to to live a decent life should they remain in it.

Saturday 2 — **"Big Haul"** The largest catch of halibut since the war was landed in Grimsby yesterday. After 3 months off the Greenland coast, a Norwegian trawler docked with 150 tons of fish, valued at £40,000.

Sunday 3 — **"Ventriloquial Rally"** New innovations at the British Ventriloquists first convention in Torquay, included a talking skull, a Toby jug, a Humpty Dumpty head, a head on a walking stick and a talking handbag.

Monday 4 — **"Centre Opened"** The vast new Soviet Exhibition Centre in Peking has been opened by the Prime Minister, Chou En-Lai. The extensive grounds surrounding the centre have been landscaped with 50,000 plants and 6,000 trees.

Tuesday 5 — **"London Dock Strike"** The strike which the National Amalgamated Stevedores and Dockers have started in London to force the port employers to negotiate with them, spread to members of the Transport and General Workers' Union. Work stopped on 72 ships, and three were undermanned.

Wednesday 6 — **"Trees to be Axed"** The seven oak trees which give the Kent town of Sevenoaks its name are to be felled and oak saplings planted in their place. The original trees came from nearby Knole Park in 1727.

Thursday 7 — **"Paris Motor Show"** Three British firms have chosen the Salon de l'Automobile to launch many new cars this year. The Hillman Husky, Sunbeam Alpine, and Vauxhall Cresta are the models making their debut.

HERE IN BRITAIN

"Recorder 'Hooks a Duck'"

A jury at Birmingham decided that the 'hook-a-duck' stall at a Birmingham fairground was not a lottery after watching the Recorder 'fish' a small blue celluloid duck from his desk. They also decided that the 'roll-'em-up' table, where pennies were rolled down ramps on to a flat table, was not a lottery either.
Of 'hook a duck', the Recorder said, *'There is skill in trying to secure any one of the ducks. Everything is as simple and ordinary a game as you have played on the vicar's lawn when bowling for a pig.'*

AROUND THE WORLD

"Present from America"

The Prime Minister, Sir Winston Churchill has been presented with a fine cigar box by the Ancient and Honourable Artillery Company of Boston, Massachusetts, in recognition of the part he has played in furthering Anglo-American friendship.

The box was made in Newburyport, Massachusetts, of silver and ebony, with a cloisonné enamel plaque on the lid, which also bears his initials and an inscription, while inside the hinged top is the Artillery Company's seal.

Cody's Pine

The site of the fatal crash into the pine tree at Farnborough airfield.

An old pine tree stands near the main entrance to the Royal Aircraft Establishment at Farnborough, close to the spot where, in May 1908, Colonel S. F. Cody made the first successful officially recorded flight in Great Britain. It has been preserved for posterity, despite it being dead for well over 30 years. The tree was killed about 1920 by oil spilt or deliberately thrown out of engines. Later, a circle of iron railings was built around the tree to support it, but by 1949 it was so rotten that a concrete plinth was cast round the trunk and the existing square of railings erected.

Last October the tree was cut down and stored until dry enough to impregnate, when the smallest pieces were soaked in a synthetic liquid resin that sets a few hours after the addition of a hardener. The larger pieces and the trunk were covered with an impervious skin wrapped around them, air was extracted by vacuum pump and liquid resin was poured through one of the pipes. After preservation had been completed the pieces of the tree were rejoined and erected on a concrete plinth so that this famous landmark will always recall that first moment of aerial history.

The plaque at his tree reads, *"Samuel Franklin Cody measured the thrust of his first aeroplane in 1908/9 by tying it to this tree and his flight of 1390 feet on 16th October 1908 was the first powered sustained flight in Great Britain."*

Cody was also a flamboyant Wild West Showman, sometimes confused with Buffalo Bill Cody whose style of dress he copied, and wore long flowing hair under a wide-brimmed cowboy hat. He arrived in England with a theatrical show in 1896 but his great interest was aviation.

Oct 8th – 4th 1954

IN THE NEWS

Friday 8 — **"Tridac"** A new analogue computer was launched at Farnborough this week, to revolutionise the development of guided weapons and fighter planes. Tridac is the world's first transistorised computer.

Saturday 9 — **"Pay for Efficiency"** An agreement for a wage increase for 400,000 railway employees has been announced by the chairman of the British Transport Commission who said he believed it would produce *'an entirely new atmosphere'*.

Sunday 10 — **"Church Support"** The anti-noise campaign in Paris has gained the support of the city's Archbishop meaning that the church bells will be rung for a shorter period, and not at all before early morning Masses.

Monday 11 — **"Late Harvest"** Due to the late spring and poor summer, much of the harvest is still being brought in with soft unripe grain that needs to be artificially dried immediately, thus inflating the cost of wheat.

Tuesday 12 — **"Unnecessary Work"** A bill is before Parliament, requesting the abolition of endorsing all cheques being paid by the recipient direct into his bank which could be costing £500,000 in extra work hours. The practice originates from 1882, when 'bills of exchange' were endorsed when transferred from one person to another.

Wednesday 13 — **"Brilliant Race for Chataway"** The Russians were victorious at the athletics match at the White City but Britain's Chris Chataway had an outstanding win in the 5,000m, beating the Russian, Kutz, and surpassing his world record by five seconds.

Thursday 14 — **"The Lion of Judah"** Haille Selassi who begins his state visit to Britain today, will be the guest of honour at a state banquet held in Buckingham Palace by Her Majesty the Queen.

HERE IN BRITAIN

"Pocket Money"

Learning the value of money starts early, often requiring a decisive choice between saving for a record or spending on sweets. Pocket money is an accepted tradition; the question is how much? A recent poll suggests a reasonable minimum of two shillings (10p) per week for twelve-year-olds.

Whilst some families link payments to housework, others establish a fair cost-of-living scale taking into account inflation in tuck and toy shops, to avoid conflict each year.

AROUND THE WORLD

"Sun Starved"

This year's vintage of German wine has been named "Soymenneclizer," meaning 'sun-starved', due to the lack of sunshine this year.

During the grape harvest festival in Neustadt, over 100,000 spectators witnessed the traditional procession make its way through the town, featuring more than 100 magnificently dressed groups and decorated floats. The event paid special tribute to Rosemarie, the wine queen of the Palatinate, and Erika the First, Germany's wine queen.

HISTORIC CATTLE

The famous wild white cattle on the Chillingham estate, Northumberland, have a new ruler of the herd. The old bull recently sought battle to preserve his dominion but was soundly defeated by a younger rival. Wild aurochs were tall, solid bovines with horns nearly 3' long, that roamed across Britain and Europe. They are the cattle depicted in prehistoric cave paintings and are the direct ancestors of all modern cattle. In Britain while these animals were gradually domesticated, some who were owned by the great landowners, such as royalty or the nobility, were kept in their natural state and allowed to remain wild in enclosed parks. As a result, there are still small herds of these pure bred native British White Cattle in existence today. Five herds are to be found at Chillingham in Northumberland, Vaynol and Dynevor in Wales, Cadzow in Lanarkshire and Woburn in Bedfordshire.

The Chillingham herd has been enclosed since the 13th century, and although numbers have fluctuated, it remains viable, with calves born each year. In 1760 the herd almost became extinct when it was reduced by an epidemic – or, some say, the bulls in the herd were reduced to three, two of which fought and killed each other, while the third was impotent - to one cow in calf, which fortunately produced a bull calf. A second occasion was in 1947, when in January of that year the herd stood at 33 head. Then came the worst winter that anyone can remember in Northumberland and by the spring no fewer than 20 of the cattle had perished. At the beginning of 1952 the herd stood at 16 head, an increase of only three in five years, and every effort is now being made to maintain numbers of this precious, and rare, breed.

Oct 15th – 21st 1954

IN THE NEWS

Friday 15 — **"Change of Title"** Following federation changes, the 'Southern Rhodesia Air Force' will change its name by permission of the Queen, to 'The Royal Rhodesian Air Force'.

Saturday 16 — **"Over 15,000 London Bus Men On Strike"** London felt the crippling effects of a third of its buses off the roads. London is usually served by 6,000 buses and 1,600 trolley buses.

Sunday 17 — **"New Exam Paper"** A new type of entrance exam has been set solely for New Hall, the all women college at Cambridge. The three-hour paper is designed to test *'logical thought and power of expression'*.

Monday 18 — **"Test Transmissions"** The BBC has announced that the new television transmission station at Rowridge on the Isle of Wight, will start making regular test transmissions as from today.

Tuesday 19 — **"Marilyn Quits"** Currently filming 'The 7 Year Itch', star Marilyn Monroe left her 2nd husband Jo DiMaggio, and filed for divorce. She and the baseball player have been married for only nine months.

Wednesday 20 — **"Pulling Out of Suez"** Britain and Egypt have agreed to end the military occupation of Suez. British forces will be fully withdrawn within 20 months.

Thursday 21 — **"Metal Fatigue"** A Westminster court of inquiry concluded that metal fatigue caused the disintegration of a pressurised cabin, causing a Comet airliner to crash off Elba in January.

HERE IN BRITAIN

"Dartmoor Ponies"

The RSPCA is making inquiries into the fate of hundreds of ponies sold annually at autumnal auctions in Dartmoor towns. Dealers explained that the keen interest displayed in recent sales was in regard to replacements for stock lost during the east coast floods, mounts for riding schools, and prospective sales to the National Coal Board.

Observers agreed that grown animals could be thus marketed, but questioned whether the high proportion of foals would end their lives in such occupations or would their carcasses eventually be described as veal on the menus of cheap restaurants or sold as meat for dogs.

AROUND THE WORLD

"Relief in Haiti"

Extensive damage has been caused by a devastating hurricane in Haiti and the response and aid efforts have been rapid. Despite severe disruption to communications, survivors reached a radio station and spread the news early in the morning.

The US Navy personnel, trained for such situations, also assisted the government in restoring communication and infrastructure. The hardest-hit areas were in the Southwest, where the impact flattened buildings, and devastated local crops. The government and the Red Cross initiated a relief operation immediately on receiving the news. The rest of the island offered voluntary assistance, donating food, clothing, transportation, and money.

Long Lasting Ink

The Book of Kells, circa 800

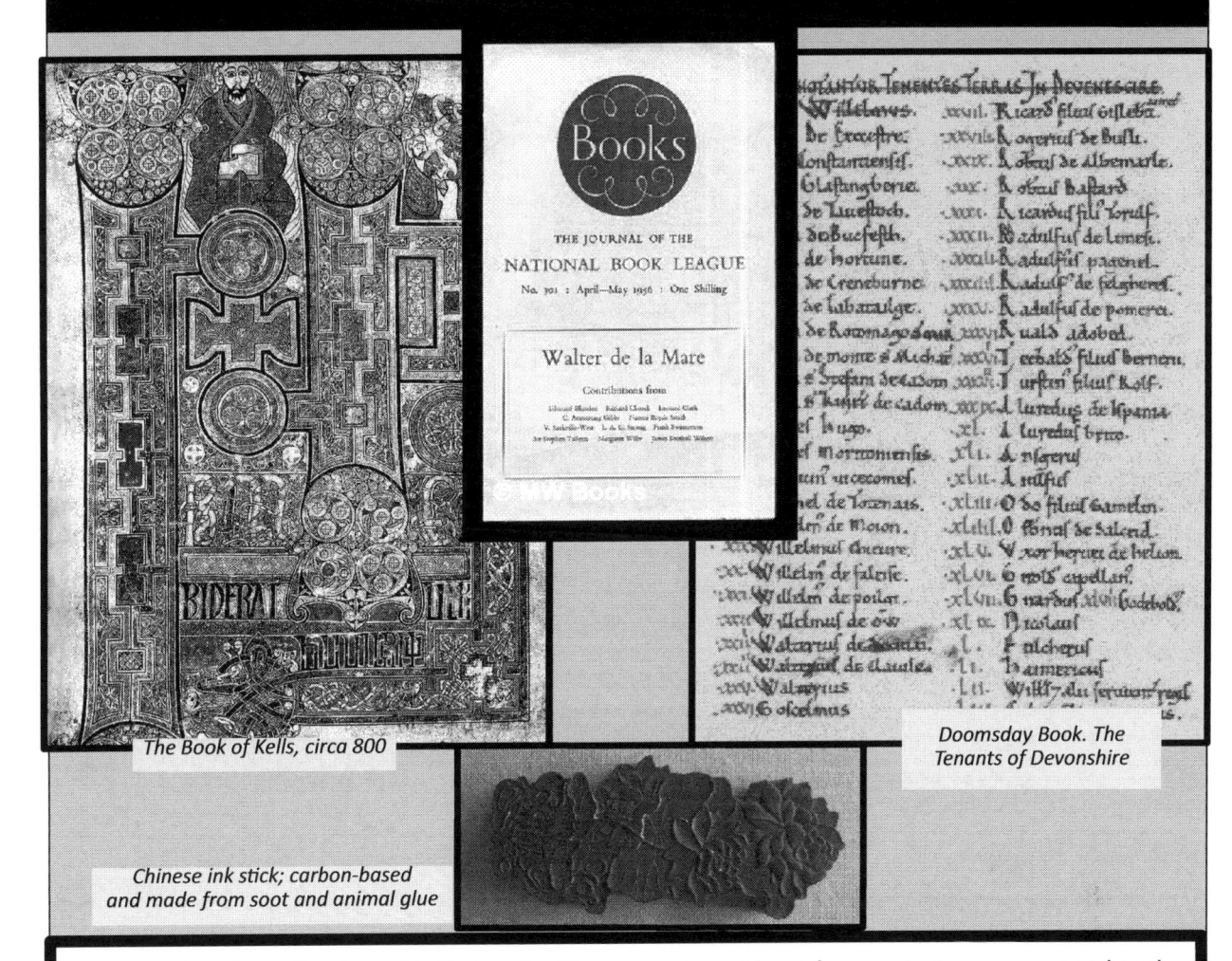

Doomsday Book. The Tenants of Devonshire

Chinese ink stick; carbon-based and made from soot and animal glue

A comprehensive collection of Italic handwriting, spanning at least four centuries, was opened at the headquarters of the National Book League this week and prompted a great deal of comment, not on the progress being made in the country by a 'handwriting campaign' but of the quality of post war ink. Regarded as 'a pale fluid that will be indecipherable in the course of time' it was compared unfavourably with examples of ancient scripts still perfectly legible after hundreds of years.

One correspondent called for an urgent campaign to restrict the use of ball point pens. *"The widespread use of these by doctors and other professional men, whose records may need to be consulted, surely demands a writing fluid which will not fade to almost complete blankness when exposed to ordinary daylight. I have seen recent medical prescriptions which could not be presented for dispensing to any chemist, lines apparently blank in hotel registers and church visitors' books, empty sheets of paper on notice boards, and signatures which have faded beyond recognition."*

Writing ink was first made over 4,000 years ago in both China and Egypt. The first inks in China were made from a mixture of lamp carbon and plant materials ground up with graphite, before being moulded into sticks and dried. This could then be reconstituted with water and applied to the paper with a brush. Some years later it was discovered that by steeping oak galls in water, and adding sulphate of iron crystals a dark, permanent writing ink was made. This was the ink that can still be read on the Dead Sea Scrolls discovered in 1947, and still graces the pages of unique and priceless documents from The Book of Kells to the Domesday Book and Magna Carta.

OCT 22ND - 28TH 1954

IN THE NEWS

Friday 22 — **"Immigration Concerns"** Birmingham City Council are to address Jamaican immigration concerns with the government. They feel the problems arise from the lack of housing and available land for building, rather than race.

Saturday 23 — **"New Pumps"** Southampton Fire Brigade have acquired eight light alloy jet pumps, developed from standard fire service equipment, which are capable of rapidly pumping out water from ships.

Sunday 24 — **"Ken John Peel"** In spite of rain and mists that blanketed the Cumbrian Fells thousands of people went to Caldbeck to pay tribute to the memory of John Peel and take part in a programme marking the centenary of his death.

Monday 25 — **"Cheap Milk"** The National Dairy Association announced that over a million people eligible for the new 'milk tokens' have failed to claim them. If they are not claimed by the end of October, the intended recipients risk paying full price.

Tuesday 26 — **"Three Sites for Independent Television"** The first three independent television stations will cover London, the Midlands, and the north, it was disclosed in a statement issued by the Independent Television Authority last night. Newspaper and cinema groups are among those to whom the first programme contracts have been offered.

Wednesday 27 — **"Saucy Play"** The licensee of a Liverpool theatre, appealed against a £10 fine for unlawfully presenting a play entitled 'The Respectable Prostitute' without the requisite permission from The Lord Chamberlain.

Thursday 28 — **"First Sea Lord"** By Royal Appointment, Admiral Lord Mountbatten will become Lord Commissioner of the Admiralty, First Sea Lord and Chief of Naval Staff from next March.

HERE IN BRITAIN

"Scottish Parliament"

A petition is to be presented to Parliament asking for a referendum on the establishment of a Scottish Parliament. The Covenant Association called for a referendum to establish a Scottish Parliament with legislative authority and resolved to petition Parliament accordingly.

The assembly also voted for the immediate establishment of a Scottish Board of Trade, independent Scottish executive authorities in nationalised industries, and accountable Ministers of State for Scottish government departments.

AROUND THE WORLD

"British Trade Fair in Iraq"

King Faisal II opened the 1st British Trade Fair to be held in Iraq. Positioned on the west bank of the River Tigris, rows of opulent pavilions house the goods of 400 British firms. Perhaps the greatest attraction for the people of Baghdad is their first chance to see television. A British firm has arranged three transmissions from the fair ground daily; these include live shows and films and a children's hour in which Iraqi children themselves will be taking part. Another unfamiliar attraction takes the form of an ice rink where two young British ballerinas will perform nightly.

PHILLUMENISTS' PASSION

The British Matchbox Label and Bookmatch Society, founded in 1948, is an International Society with members interested in matchboxes, matchbox labels, book match covers and all types of match related items from around the globe. Many members are also interested in the match making industry, the social history of match making, match related ephemera and graphic art design and like all collectors, they are men of devotion and passion. The society puts out a bi-monthly newsletter and holds six well attended rallies a year in London.

This week, at their annual exhibition, old friends were reunited, financial transactions made and information exchanged. Some enthusiasts base their collection on a single theme such as flora and fauna, while others concentrate on the designs of one country, such as Spain or Austria. Label subjects vary enormously; there is a whole Spanish series of the etchings of Goya, labels showing royalty of many countries, actresses, shipping, air and railway lines, sports and pastimes, nature reserves, national costumes, panoramas, and much else. The exhibition itself goes far enough to show that match-box label collecting can be a life's work.

The society secretary, to mention only one, has a set of 45,000 different pieces: but that scarcely vies with the collection of an American who has a collection of 120,000 pieces. American designs are much sought after, particularly Troy labels which can command higher values than say those of British origin. What upsets the British phillumenists is that they feel they cannot take pride in our own national match-box labels, 'British labels are awful', said one member with much feeling, and while that may not be entirely true, it has to be said that many of the foreign examples are so detailed and colourful that they can easily put our more utilitarian offerings in the shade.

OCT 29TH – NOV 4TH 1954

IN THE NEWS

Friday 29 — **"Heavy Floods in Scotland"** Road and railway bridges were washed away, express trains were delayed, roads were blocked, thousands of acres of farmland were under water and village streets were inundated by floods which followed heavy rain in southern Scotland and northern England yesterday.

Saturday 30 — **"Commemorative Plaque"** The Franco-British Society chairman unveiled a plaque at the French Embassy, in London, marking the 50th anniversary of the Entente Cordiale.

Sunday 31 — **"Fair Swap?"** Two mothers given the wrong babies in a mix-up at Forest Gate Hospital six weeks ago, have been given their 'own' babies now and will decide after a 24-hour trial period if the exchange should be permanent.

Monday Nov 1 — **"Dockers Back Today"** Work was resumed by the 44,000 men who have been idle at eight ports holding up imports and exports valued at some £200m in the worst dock strike since 1945.

Tuesday 2 — **"Everybody Out Again"** Nearly 2,500 dock employees stopped work *unofficially* in London when workers refused to load goods on to lorries driven by men who did not belong to a union, or who were said to have accepted goods from ships during the strike.

Wednesday 3 — **"King George VI Fund"** Queen Elizabeth the Queen Mother was the guest of honour at a dinner attended by 3,000 people at the English-Speaking Union in New York. The Queen acknowledged the recent establishment of their fund in memory of her late husband.

Thursday 4 — **"American Expelled"** An American diplomat's wife will leave Russia with her husband tomorrow, according to the embassy. She is accused of hooliganism after slapping a Russian who tried to detain her.

HERE IN BRITAIN

"Saved for Posterity"

A rare fairground organ built in 1909 has been acquired by a band of enthusiasts in Durham, where it is being restored to be used to raise money for charity. The organ is probably the largest ever built for fairground use, a Gavioli, it was originally built with 110 keys for a bioscope show at Erith.
In 1918 it was cut down to 98 keys and fitted into a Welsh scenic railway. Last September the owner, a showman, donated it to the group. The organ weighs between 8-10 tons, is 28ft. long, 8ft. 3in. wide, and 13ft. 6in. high.

AROUND THE WORLD

"Horror Comics"

In New York, to eliminate so-called 'comic books' that revel in sadism, sex, and the more sordid activities of life, the Comic Magazine Association of America, has announced a set of rules for publishers. They prohibit any presentation that creates sympathy or glorification of the criminal; weapons; excessive violence, kidnapping; use of 'horror' and 'terror,' and attacks on religion or race. The code also sets standards for dress. 'Females' it states, 'shall always be drawn realistically, without any exaggeration of any physical qualities.'

COLCHESTER OYSTERS

The River Colne Near Colchester

A galaxy of distinguished visitors attended the Colchester Oyster Feast this week. Lord Hailsham, Q.C., lead the customary tributes, and as the proposer of a toast dedicated simply and exclusively to 'The Oyster', described the oyster '*as luscious, succulent, invigorating, not too expensive, and still happily immune from the art of the English cook.*' As for the Colchester oyster, he considered it '*the monarch of oysters, the emperor of bivalves, and the head of the whole commonwealth of shellfish*'. Sir Andrew Clark, Q.C., responding, said that it was clearly his duty to speak for the oysters that had been consumed at the feast, '*for they achieved distinction in such company as assembled for this occasion. Those eaten by the several bishops present for example, might find consolation in being received into the very bosom of the Church*'.

Earlier in the week, with three cheers for the Queen and the traditional gin and gingerbread as an appetiser, the first Colchester native oysters of the new season were dredged and eaten in their bed in the Pyefleet Creek. The burgesses of Colchester have held the right to fish the Colne for oysters '*from time beyond which memory runneth not to the contrary*'. The Town Clerk read to the corporation and the fishermen gathered on the Native the proclamation first made on this same water in 1256, whereby '*our very excellent Lord King*' Henry III confirmed the burgesses in their right and forbade poaching under pain of forfeiture and grievous amercements.' In Tudor times, Colchester 'natives' were given as 'gifts' from the local authority to the Sovereign or their Courtiers if they visited the town, often allowing the Borough benefits in return and up to the start of the Great War, the Natives appeared on the tables of the rich and powerful across the world.

Nov 5th - 1st 1954

IN THE NEWS

Friday 5 — **"Under the Sea"** As part of a regeneration programme to expand production, a 1,700ft. shaft will be sunk at the Wearmouth Colliery, in Sunderland. The current mine workings extend three miles out to sea.

Saturday 6 — **"Unscrupulous Amateurs"** Too many unqualified individuals openly posing as auctioneers and estate agents is a cause for concern according to the Chartered Auctioneers' and Estate Agents' Institute.

Sunday 7 — **"Homage Led by the Queen"** The Queen, dressed in black relieved only by a poppy, was at the Cenotaph to lay a wreath after the Two Minutes Silence of remembrance. The Duke of Edinburgh and the Duke of Gloucester, who stood behind the Queen, also laid wreaths, and one was placed for Queen Elizabeth the Queen Mother, who is in America.

Monday 8 — **"The Bath of America"** Annapolis turned out to give Queen Elizabeth the Queen Mother a royal welcome tinged with memories of the time when the city had close connections with the Crown. On the way to the Governor's mansion, she passed signposts to 'Epping Forest' and 'Sherwood Forest.'

Tuesday 9 — **"Plea to the Vatican"** In order to prevent a move recognising Jerusalem as Israel's capital, Lebanon have appealed to the Pope, asking him to influence on the Western leaders.

Wednesday 10 — **"Aid to Germany"** The Committee for American Relief in Europe will be providing 155,000 Christmas food parcels to poverty-stricken Berlin families who are in desperate need.

Thursday 11 — **"Flu Jabs"** 16,000 volunteers this winter will participate in trials organised by the Ministry of Health, to test four influenza vaccines which have been produced in Britain.

HERE IN BRITAIN

"The Lord Mayors Show'"

This week saw a change of Lord Mayor of London. Since the 13th century the newly elected mayor makes his way through London by coach to swear loyalty to the monarch.

The mayor receives a blessing at St. Paul's and proceeds to The Courts of Justice where the oath is taken. The Livery Companies, Police and Armed Forces are represented, and traditional uniforms are worn. It is a mixture of pageantry and carnival, a celebration of the City's ancient power and prosperity, just as the parades of centuries past.

AROUND THE WORLD

"National Church'"

Washington's Cathedral of St. Peter and St. Paul, although known in America as The National Church, has many tangible connections with Britain. The pulpit was made by stonemasons at Canterbury from cathedral stone. The bishop's chair is made of stone from Glastonbury, whilst in the surrounding garden are stones from Whitby Abbey and a sundial and oak tree from England.

This week, Queen Elizabeth the Queen Mother attended a Memorial Service of Matin to remember the fallen of both our nations in two World Wars.

FASHIONABLE BLENHEIM

Blenheim Palace is one of the jewels in Britain's historical crown, a lavish gift from a grateful Queen Anne to John Churchill, 1st Duke of Marlborough for his military triumphs, and his ruthless, socially ambitious wife. Blenheim, the only non-royal, non-episcopal country house in England to hold the title of 'palace', is graceful, elegant and above all else, spectacular. This week it was the setting for a fashion show which presented the creations of fashion's doyen, Christian Dior, to members of high society. The Duchess of Marlborough, who is a member of the Red Cross Council, lent her home for the evening as the host for a lavish fashion show to help raise money for The British Red Cross Society.

Special lighting transformed the rooms into an opulent fashion salon to showcase Dior's latest winter collection. The catwalk started in the Coral Room in the west wing and from there, the mannequins walked down the Long Library, where Princess Margaret was guest of honour, through the state rooms hung with the tapestries depicting Marlborough's famous battle victories in the 18th century, into the green and red drawing rooms, culminating in the Grand Cabinet which is dominated by Romney's portrait of the fashionable 4th Duchess of Marlborough.

As might be expected in such a prestigious setting, the gowns were stunning, each set to background music played on the organ in the library and relayed through all nine rooms. Chopin's 'Les Sylphides' for the short ballerina style cocktail dresses overlaid with lace, Debussy's 'Claire de Lune' for the full-length evening gowns. Although hints of Dior's 'New Look' still remain, also featured were pencil thin skirts and full peplumed jackets. One ensemble called simply 'The Blenheim', was raffled, and the proceeds added to the £9,000 already raised for the charity by the evening.

Nov 12th - 18th 1954

IN THE NEWS

Friday 12   **"Caxton's Memorial"** A stone tablet was unveiled at Westminster Abbey in memory of William Caxton, the first English printer. He set up his printing press in England in 1477 in the vicinity of the abbey.

Saturday 13   **"Seven Breaches in Trent Banks"** Abnormally high tides caused serious floods on the east coast. The damage was most severe at Kingston-upon-Hull, where the river overflowed and inundated a large area of the town.

Sunday 14   **"Russian Orders"** The Russian Government, who hold the view that religious belief retards the building of Communism, have nevertheless now instructed officials to treat clergy respectfully.

Monday 15   **"Arctic Air Route Inauguration"** The first commercial service across the Arctic from Europe to the west coast of North America began by SAS from Copenhagen.

Tuesday 16   **"Parking Restrictions"** The Minister of Transport has conceded that it is neither just nor practicable to prohibit the entry of private cars into central London, but in order to keep traffic moving the present unilateral waiting and no-waiting restrictions are to be substantially extended and parking meters introduced.

Wednesday 17   **"Tube Comfort"** The first tube train car to be sprung using rubber-cushioning materials for greater comfort, went into service on the Piccadilly Line.

Thursday 18   **"Tribunal Award to Footplate Men"** Increases in pay ranging from 13s. to £1 6s. (65p to £1.30) a week have been awarded to nearly 83,000 railway locomotive drivers. Increases for firemen range from 5s. to 19s. 6d (25p to 97p).

HERE IN BRITAIN

"London to Brighton Crush"

The combination of a sunny autumn day and the annual RAC veteran car run on Sunday produced acute traffic congestion on the London to Brighton road, the ordinary motorist taking about five hours to complete the 56 mile journey.

Most motorists kept in single file, to give the old cars a free run, and 182 of the 212 starters completed their journey within the specified time. Despite an early start, the road in Hyde Park quickly became choked with spectators' cars and often, along the route, there was only just room for the veterans to pass between the crowds of spectators.

AROUND THE WORLD

"Beetle Treason"

The Colorado beetle is depicted by Communist propaganda as the favourite agent of the 'American Imperialists' for sabotaging the people's potato crop. Now a Czechoslovak Government botanist has been sentenced to 20 years' imprisonment for high treason and sabotage.

Among the offences that he admitted were breeding Colorado beetles in a preserving jar and spreading them in fields. In the past, Communist propaganda has alleged that Colorado beetles were dropped from American aircraft.

ELLIS ISLAND CLOSED

Seen from east. From left to right: contagious diseases ward; lawn; hospital; ferry basin; main building, kitchen, dormitory, and immigration building. The inset shows the main entrance.

America's iconic immigration and detention centre on Ellis Island, offshore from New York, closed this week after being in constant service for 62 years. This follows a relaxing of the country's policy on its immigration rules, and reduction of the detention period for those needing to be deported back to their own country. Until the facility was opened in 1892, each individual state had been responsible for implementing the immigration process, but the first person to pass through the new federal system in January of that year was a 15-year-old Irish girl, travelling with her two brothers, in search of opportunity and a better future. With 1st and 2nd class passengers being subjected to a much briefer inspection on board their ships, third class passengers disembarked onto the island for rigorous medical, legal and rudimentary intelligence testing to ascertain their suitability for immigration. This could take as much as 7 hours and up to 2% of arrivals were sent back at this stage.

The complex of buildings rapidly expanded to include barracks, laundry and kitchen, as well as medical facilities and a hospital to deal with and isolate those with contagious diseases. Despite its size it was never large enough to handle the hundreds of thousands of immigrants and often people were detained on board their transatlantic ships for days due to backlogs in processing. In 1924, a change in legislation meant that Ellis Island became purely a detention and deportation centre for illegal immigrants. In WWII it was used by the army as a detention centre for prisoners of war, a military hospital and U.S. Coast Guard training centre. The last person to be processed there recently was a Norwegian seaman who had overstayed his shore leave and was deported back to Norway. There are currently no plans for the facility to be re-used for other purposes.

Nov 19th - 25th 1954

IN THE NEWS

Friday 19 — **"Four Day Influenza"** Thousands of children in the north and west of England are ill with running noses, sore throats, and feverish temperatures, closing many schools.

Saturday 20 — **"Low Standards"** Birmingham Clean Food Guild, formed to raise food standards, has closed after just one year due to poor support from the City's 15,000 traders. Of 14 applicants, only 5 met minimum hygiene standards.

Sunday 21 — **"Immigration Centres"** Lambeth Council are to request the Colonial Office for transit and reception centres to be set up to accommodate the increasing numbers of West Indians immigrants arriving in Britain.

Monday 22 — **"Big Order"** The Cycle and Motorcycle show closed with orders for 1,000 bicycles from Pakistan and an order for 2,000 scooters from Sweden, with more orders promised.

Tuesday 23 — **"Import records"** The global rise in meat production last year led to a significant influx of imports into the UK, the world's largest importer. Britain imported nearly 1.3 million tons of meat.

Wednesday 24 — **"Prima Facie Case"** The extradition proceedings against the seven Polish seamen who sought political asylum after their trawler put into port at Whitby on September 23 were concluded with all the men committed on a charge of revolt against the master of a ship on the high seas.

Thursday 25 — **"Prorogation of Parliament"** The long 1953-54 session, opened by the Queen on November 3, 1953, was ended by prorogation. After an interval of five days, the Queen will go to Westminster again on November 30 to open the new session.

HERE IN BRITAIN

"Guildhall Restored"

Restoration of the war damage to Guildhall, in the City of London, is finished and it is open to the public. The architect in charge of the work believes that the medieval roof had either stone arches or a stone vault, the clustered stone columns not being the proper form of support for a timber hammer-beam roof, like the one destroyed in 1940, and has therefore reconstructed the roof with stone arches.

He has also designed new panelling for the hall, a double row of candelabra in bronze and new stained glass for the windows.

AROUND THE WORLD

"Onassis Defies Ban"

Mr. Onassis, the Greek-born shipping magnate, has challenged the Peruvian Government over the prohibition of whaling within 200 miles of the Peruvian coast. His Olympic Maritime company's whaling fleet, comprising 16 whalers and one factory ship, has caught whales within this limit. Threats that the Peruvian Navy would fire on ships found fishing within the 200 miles, has not been carried out. Mr. Onassis's protest follows Chile, Ecuador, and Peru recently signing an agreement declaring their territorial waters should extend 200 miles from the coast, to protect sea life.

Mail Order Shopping

In the years following the end of the war, retail sales of personal and household goods through catalogue firms have risen sharply, with companies such as Grattan, and Freemans recording significant year end profits. The post-war boom has seen upwards of 7,000 parcels a day being dispatched, most being paid for by weekly instalments as laid out in a hire purchase agreement, known colloquially as the 'Never-Never'. This name comes from the common feeling that you can never pay off the debt and will never own the item you are paying for. Due to the high interest charges, the payment period could be up to a year longer than just paying the purchase price weekly.

Freemans and Littlewoods can compete with the large department stores in the range and quality of goods offered for sale, and designated agents lend out the large catalogues to friends and family and manage the ordering and collecting of monthly payments. While this responsibility earns them discount off their own purchases, any bad debts also become the agent's liability. The rehousing programme since the war has meant that many people have been moved to suburbs far away from the familiar high streets and markets. Now, not only does this new form of retail offer a chance to spread the cost of more expensive goods over a period of time, but such is the purchasing power of the catalogue companies, that often a wider range of merchandise can be offered to the customer than would be found in high street shops.

Mail order shopping was inspired by a little-known 19th Century Welsh draper who lived 'in the middle of nowhere' in rural mid-Wales and left school at 12. Pryce Jones set up his business and his customers for Welsh flannel included Queen Victoria and Florence Nightingale.

Nov 26th – Dec 2nd 1954

IN THE NEWS

Friday 26 — **"Cable to Span Atlantic"** Production of the first transatlantic telephone cable has begun at a new factory in Erith, specially built for the purpose at a cost of over £1m.

Saturday 27 — **"Serious Flooding in the West and Midlands"** A combination of gales and more heavy rain caused further widespread flooding. There were winds of up to 78 m.p.h. and an inch of rain fell for the second successive day in parts of Devon and Cornwall. In 13 counties, 51 important roads were impassable or seriously flooded.

Sunday 28 — **"Hot Wax"** Molten wax from a candle factory fire flooded the streets and sewers of Otley in Yorkshire. 20 tons of sandbags were used to barricade the street to stop the wax from reaching the main residential area of town.

Monday 29 — **"The Ark"** The Royal Navy has come to the aid of a German circus stranded in Malta. 'Operation Noah's Ark' has provided two landing craft and begun to transport the animals, equipment and 135 staff, to their next destination in Sicily.

Tuesday 30 — **"Sir Winston's Birthday"** The Prime Minister celebrated his 80th birthday with a day of presentations and tributes. 2,500 people, including cabinet ministers and opposition leaders, filled Westminster Hall for the televised ceremony.

Wed Dec 1 — **"Appeal Successful"** The seven Polish seamen from the trawler Puszczyk, were released from prison after a week, following an appeal against their extradition. All declared that they would like to join British ships.

Thursday 2 — **"Travel Concessions"** Birmingham City Council are to appeal to the House of Lords against a ruling forbidding them to offer free or reduced travel fares to old people.

HERE IN BRITAIN

"Farewell to Blanco"

British soldiers at home stations are now using their last cakes of 'Blanco' because by Christmas they will be using a new product which looks and is applied rather like boot polish, with a brush but without water. Blanco has been the officially recognized cleaner for items of uniform made of webbing since 1913, but the search for a substitute has been ongoing for some time.

It is claimed that the new renovator, which will be sold exclusively by the NAAFI, is easy to apply, dries quickly, does not rub off, is long lasting, and can be touched up or just wiped over.

AROUND THE WORLD

"Thanksgiving Turkey"

Some five million turkeys will be eaten this year by citizens of the United States celebrating Thanksgiving Day, the traditional festival dating back to 1621 when the Pilgrim Fathers gave thanks to God for their first successful harvest in North America.

According to historical records the pilgrims ate 'wild fowl' which could indeed have been wild turkeys, similar in size to the domesticated birds. Although it is not certain that turkey was eaten on the first ever Thanksgiving, it is firmly established now as part of the tradition, along with sweet potato, cornbread and pecan pie.

Winston Churchill

A painting by Churchill

Churchill (centre) commanding the 6th Battalion, the Royal Scots Fusiliers, 1916.

Britain's Prime Minister, Sir Winston Churchill, was the first to celebrate his 80th birthday in office this week. Born on November 30th 1874 at Blenheim Palace, he has already lived through the reigns of five monarchs. He has served his country in the army for twenty-nine years and was decorated five times, having fought in some of the most notorious engagements in the late 19th century, particularly in The Boer War. His parliamentary career began in 1899 and so far, has spanned 61 years, with numerous ministerial posts prior to becoming Prime Minister for the first time in 1940. It was in this particular term of office during the Second World War that Churchill became such an iconic figure on the world stage, inspiring and encouraging the Allied Troops to final victory in 1945.

Often outspoken and dogmatic, he is the epitome of the British spirit of grit and determination. It was during the war that his skill as an orator came to the fore, making full use of radio to broadcast his inspiring words to a war weary Europe. He held onto his vision that after the war there needed to be a 'United States of Europe' which would include a renewed Germany, whilst at the same time building on and strengthening the bonds forged between America and Britain both during and after the conflict. However, he is as much a master of the written as the spoken word, having written many books, both reference and fiction, last year being awarded the Nobel Prize for Literature.

His other interest is painting - a passion which first developed in 1915, and continues to this day, and although he exhibited at the Royal Society of Portrait Painters in 1919, he is far more self-deprecating about this work than his writing, calling them *'mere daubs'*.

Dec 3rd – 9th 1954

IN THE NEWS

Friday 3 — **"Flagship visits London"** The Commander-in-Chief of the Home Fleet brought his flagship, HMS Apollo, up to the Pool of London, the largest warship ever to steam so far up the Thames.

Saturday 4 — **"Call to Raise Pension Age"** The Phillips committee set up in 1953 has recommended because of the increasing cost of old age pensions that the minimum age for claiming national pensions should be raised from 65 to 68 for men and from 60 to 63 for women.

Sunday 5 — **"Power to Heal"** An eminent St. Bartholomew's Hospital psychiatrist has probed 100 cases of 'paranormal' healing and suggests there is potential for it to have the power to influence the course of disease.

Monday 6 — **"Elusive Otter"** An otter was chased by police and passers-by through the streets of Cleethorpes in Lincolnshire for four hours, scattering crowds and causing cars to swerve. It was eventually caught by the R.S.P.C.A. and released in the countryside.

Tuesday 7 — **"Christmas Appeal"** The Manchester Union of Postal Workers have appealed to football pools firms to cancel coupons for matches to be played on December 25th, as the volume of mail it produces may compromise Christmas deliveries.

Wednesday 8 — **"Radioactive Medicine"** A vehicle carrying radioactive chlorine travelled from the Berkshire atomic energy plant at Harwell, to Leeds Infirmary, with a police escort. Radioactive chemicals are being used in a research programme at Leeds University.

Thursday 9 — **"Bumper Catch"** So far during this autumn's fishing season, a total of 33,000 barrels of cured herring have been exported from Great Yarmouth, bound for Russia.

HERE IN BRITAIN

"The Missing Bob"

At Loughborough, eight bell ringers set out to fulfil the ambition of campanologists - to ring all the combinations of, and permutations possible on, eight bells, a feat requiring each man to pull his rope 40,320 times in the right order for about 20 hours.

They used light bells and new ropes in the campanile of a bell foundry, insulated, with locked doors, whitewashed windows and soundproofed. But when they were just a few hundred changes short of the record of 21,600, they suddenly ended. The conductor mistakenly ordered a 'stand', the traditional ending of a peal, instead of a 'bob'.

AROUND THE WORLD

"Food Research"

A recent report examined the benefits of white flour versus whole wheat flour, focusing on trials conducted in Germany. The study found that growth of children aged 5 to 15 were similar regardless of whether they received whole wheat flour, white flour, or white flour enriched with B vitamins and iron. Two orphanages participated, one relying heavily on bread and vegetables for energy while the other incorporated bread, fat, and sugar into the diet. The results were consistent in both cases. After a year, a pint of milk was added daily for six months, but contrary to previous tests, this did not lead to improved growth.

CRYSTAL PALACE

The Crystal Palace in Hyde Park, London, in 1851 and when relocated to Sydenham (Inset).

The original Crystal Palace was created from cast iron and plate glass to a design by Joseph Paxton, to house The Great Exhibition of 1851. The brainchild of Prince Albert, Queen Victoria's husband, the exhibition was designed to showcase the best creations of trade and industry at that time and attracted visitors from all over the world. Taking only nine months from start to finish, it was large enough to display the 14,000 exhibits of produce and large-scale machinery, as well as fully grown trees which were part of the landscape of Hyde Park where it was built.

Over six million visitors were counted at the toll gates over the month that it was open to the public. After the exhibition closed the structure remained in place until it was carefully taken down, and rebuilt and modified on top of Sydenham Hill, on the Surrey - Kent border. With exhibition halls, a full-sized concert hall showcasing a 4,000-piece orchestra, and state of the art facilities it was officially opened in 1854. During WW1 it became a naval training establishment, known as HMS Crystal Palace.

However, its popularity waned over the years, and one night in 1936 a small fire quickly spread in high winds, and despite the efforts of over 400 fire fighters, by morning all that was left was a smouldering ruin. The site has remained in use however for outdoor activities and there are now plans to develop it as a national youth and sports centre, with a hall, all weather facilities, running tracks and stands for spectators, a general open-air practice area of some three acres and a swimming pool, all built to Olympic standards. It was emphasised this week that the proposed centre would be concerned exclusively with amateur sport, having as its main purpose the training of trainers.

Dec 10th – 6th 1954

IN THE NEWS

Friday 10 — **"Court Martial Monty"** An indignant Prime Minister flatly refused an MP's request that Field Marshal Montgomery should be court-martialled under the Official Secrets Act, following disclosure of secret documents from Churchill.

Saturday 11 — **"Air Pollution Costs"** The British Electricity Authority stated that equipment installation at power stations to limit air pollution could cost between £140m and £250m over 10 years.

Sunday 12 — **"Biting Question"** At a Conservative Party meeting in Scotland, one voter demanded to know what the government proposed to do about the midge swarms that make life intolerable in summer?

Monday 13 — **"Rescue Operation"** The army in Eire has been mobilised to help in Dublin, where almost a thousand families have been made temporarily homeless by floods from the Tolka river. 40 square miles are under water and the Army took over rescue work. The homeless are being fed from field kitchens and accommodated in huts at Athlone.

Tuesday 14 — **"Family Allowance"** The National Federation of Class Teachers have called for the misuse of family allowances to be investigated. There are claims of no improvement in children's diet or conditions amongst some of the families receiving the money.

Wednesday 15 — **"Scottish Bridge Hopes Dashed"** Government recommendation for the funding loan scheme proposed by Lord Teviot was rejected delaying again the long-awaited road bridge over the Firth of Forth.

Thursday 16 — **"Submarine Disaster"** Three men were believed last night to have lost their lives when the submarine Talent was swept out of her dock at Chatham after a caisson had collapsed, causing an inrush of water.

HERE IN BRITAIN

"Major Reconstruction"

A proposal has been put before the Ministry of Works for the raising of one of the trilithons at Stonehenge, which has been collapsed on the ground, under 3 other very large stones, since 1797. Such an exercise would give unprecedented opportunities to examine the stones in detail to determine why they fell, and what is on the underside of the stones, or indeed what lies buried beneath them? The trilithons are the sets of 3 stones - 2 tall uprights, and the 3rd crossbar which lies on the top of them, secured by a mortice and tenon joint carved into the stone.

AROUND THE WORLD

"Paris Marathon"

A laboratory car, 'Genevieve', has completed a cruise of 100 days in Paris traffic, during which it has been driven 20 hours a day and covered over 60,000 miles. Genevieve - the name is a tribute to the immense popularity in France of the recent British film - was commissioned to make a scientific study of Paris traffic conditions from the point of view of the driver. For 2,000 hours driving, 266 million engine revolutions, over 203,448 applications of the foot brake, and some 185,000 changes of gear were recorded. The motor horn was used an average of 600 times a day.

KNOTTY PROBLEMS

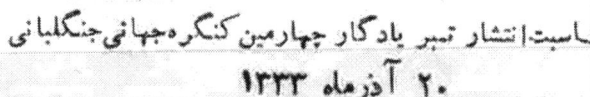

4 Th FORESTS PROTECT
International Conferance
11 Th December 1954

The 4th World Forestry Congress is to be hosted by India this year and will focus in particular on the problems of tropical forestry. The bulk of the timber trade is supplied with 'softwoods' such as pine, larch, and spruce from Northern Europe, Russia and Canada. Broad leaved 'hardwood' trees such as oak, ash, beech and maple grow in areas which have been largely set aside for agriculture, such as Central Europe and North America. This zone has the highest density of population, so timber is usually for local consumption rather than for trade.

Tropical forest reaches its maximum development in the Amazon basin and Central Africa and large areas of south-east Asia, New Guinea, and north-east Australia. Not much is known about the extent of this forestry area, what timber is available, timber production or current activities affecting the areas, but it is believed there is enormous scope for improvement in tropical forestry including methods of creating new forests where the original trees have been destroyed. However, much of the forest is growing on land that could be used for food crops, including many timbered swamps that may one day have to be used to produce rice, thus the increasing demands for land for food production are steadily reducing the area usable for afforestation.

In Britain, after the devastation of the last war, the Forestry Commission was set up in 1919, with power to acquire land for afforestation. The Government is pursuing a vigorous forestry policy asking that the nation devotes 5,000,000 acres - approximately one-eleventh of the total land area - to forest by the end of the century to ensure national safety and reasonable insurance against future shortages in world supplies.

Dec 17th - 23rd 1954

IN THE NEWS

Friday 17 — **"Search for Bomber Abandoned"** An intensive search for a missing R.A.F. Lancaster bomber with a crew of seven which crashed into the sea 50 miles south-west of the Scilly Isles was called off. Ships had reported an explosion and sflames in the area and two bodies and some wreckage were recovered by the British destroyer Barrosa.

Saturday 18 — **"Bill Without Precedent"** Mr. Anthony Wedgwood Benn, Labour M.P. and heir to Lord Stansgate, is seeking to renounce his right of succession to the viscounty by means of an unprecedented Personal Bill in the House of Lords.

Sunday 19 — **"Cookery Classes"** Derbyshire's East Midlands Electricity Board are offering cookery lessons for blind housewives, using cookers with controls in Braille and bells which warn when food is cooked.

Monday 20 — **"School at Sea"** At Hastings, the unusual spectacle of a school of porpoises swimming close to shore in calm seas, drew large crowds to the sea front to watch.

Tuesday 21 — **"Christmas Message"** The Secretary of State for War, in a Christmas message to all ranks of the British Army said, *'We hope that redeployment in the Middle East, withdrawal of the Trieste Garrison and of our Forces in Korea, will bring greater stability in the Army and a higher proportion of troops at home.'*

Wednesday 22 — **"Christmas Cheer"** A consignment of Jamaica rum has been sent to the Mayor of Kingston-on-Thames, from Kingston, Jamaica so they can make a Christmas punch for the city fathers' Christmas celebrations.

Thursday 23 — **"More Passengers, Fewer Flights"** BEA are using larger aircraft this year and expect to carry about 25% more Continental passengers than last Christmas on about 15% fewer flights. Some 10,000 people will be carried during December 21-24, mainly on Viscount and Elizabethan aircraft, which have replaced the small Vikings.

HERE IN BRITAIN
"Guga Off the Menu"

The people of Ness on Lewis are up in arms since realising that the Protection of Birds Act, 1954, prohibits them from killing and eating the solan goose, or guga, as they call it in Gaelic.
In 1549 Dean Munro recorded that the people of Ness paid an annual visit to Sula Sgeir -a rocky islet lying 30 miles north of the Bust of Lewis - and *'fetch hame with them their boitt full of dray wild foulis, with wyld foulis fedders.'* How long before his day the custom began no one can say, but it has continued ever since.

AROUND THE WORLD
"Like Father, Like Son"

Dag Hammarskjold has followed his father in taking his seat in the Swedish Academy. He become one of 'The Eighteen' when he delivered an account of the life and works of his late father, Hjalmar Hammarskjold, who was Prime Minister of Sweden during the First World War.
The Academy is the guardian of the annual Nobel award for literature and membership is made up of scholars, scientists, authors and men prominent in public affairs.

CHRISTMAS BOUNTY

With rationing at an end and fewer import restrictions than at any time since before the war, the display of food in the shops this month is redolent of a Dickens novel. There is a cornucopia of tempting foods to complement those mainstays of the season's menu - the turkey and the Christmas pudding. In the last few years many foods have been substituted or done without, but this year there is everything in the way of seasonal or luxurious additions to put on the table. Exotic treats such as crystallised fruits, or pate de foie gras are in plentiful supply.

As all the raw ingredients are easily available, there are fewer ready-made cakes, puddings and mince pies, allowing the housewives to show off their prowess in the kitchen and for the first time, locally cured hams are unrationed and, although expensive at 6s 4d per lb, (30p/kg) are proving very popular. More than one grocer has already sold out of the limited stock they had prepared and are relying on tinned hams to fulfil late orders.

Another sign of a return to pre-war choice is a return to lavishness in packaging, from chocolates in wooden boxes, to stuffed dates in porcelain dishes which can be used long after the fruits have been eaten. Tins of sweets or biscuits, are always popular, decorated with artistic designs, some 'by courtesy of the trustees of the National Gallery'. This year in particular, tea is proving popular, because the high price makes it something of a luxury. The choice ranges from large canisters of exotic blends like Lapsang Souchong, to small quantities of Breakfast Tea in pottery jugs. There is something on offer for everyone, promising a welcome return to Christmases of former years.

Dec 24th - 31st 1954

IN THE NEWS

Friday 24 — **"Larger cards"** The fashion for sending larger greetings cards is creating problems for the Post Office as only half the number of these larger cards fit into a mailbag and more vans are needed to carry them.

Saturday 25 — **"Queen's Message"** The Queen made her broadcast from her study at Sandringham, Norfolk. Her Majesty and the Duke of Edinburgh spent the festivities with their children.

Sunday 26 — **"Walk to Freedom"** A refugee from a detention camp in East Germany escaped from his police escort on December 18th and has walked the 130 miles to West Germany.

Monday 27 — **"Comic Football"** Three thousand people watched the annual match between fishermen and ships' firemen on the south sands at Scarborough. After one of the players had been thrown into the sea, the firemen were declared the winners.

Tuesday 28 — **"Roman Ruins"** A small, 1st century columbarium, which was a Roman sepulchre for cremation urns, has been unearthed at an archaeological site near Colchester.

Wednesday 29 — **"Christmas Cubs"** Six tiger cubs have been born in Edinburgh Zoo. All are doing well but three have been removed from their mother because of the size of the litter.

Thursday 30 — **"Training Underwater"** Two small, five-man training submarines launched in Cumbria are named 'Stickleback' and 'Shrimp'.

Friday 31st — **"A Wee Dram"** Customs were bemused when a ship which had left London five months earlier, docked with a cargo of fine old whisky. It's 30,000-mile round trip is just part of a secret maturing process.

HERE IN BRITAIN

"Christmas Money'"

New coins at Christmas are eagerly sought. Although since 1947 'silver' coins have been made of cupro-nickel, the copper content of the sixpence won't stop them being put in the Christmas pudding but again there will be no new pennies. Since WW1 the issue of pennies has been intermittent with none at all since 1949. The farthing, bright and golden as a new penny, is always in demand for use as counters for Christmas games and the ideal coin for a tradesman's gift on Boxing Day, is the grand five-shilling crown, but none have been struck this year.

AROUND THE WORLD

"Silver Dollars"

There is always a demand for 'Cartwheels', as silver dollars were called, as gifts. The US Mint in Philadelphia unwittingly put three million rare 'Liberty Head' Cartwheels into circulation this week, each coin being worth between $2 and $17 to collectors depending on its age. They were originally minted at the beginning of the century to back the issue of paper dollars which promised redemption with silver dollars. Later the promise on the notes was changed to read 'payable in silver' without designating any specific coin. Because of that, few of the earlier minted dollars went into circulation.

Toys For Christmas

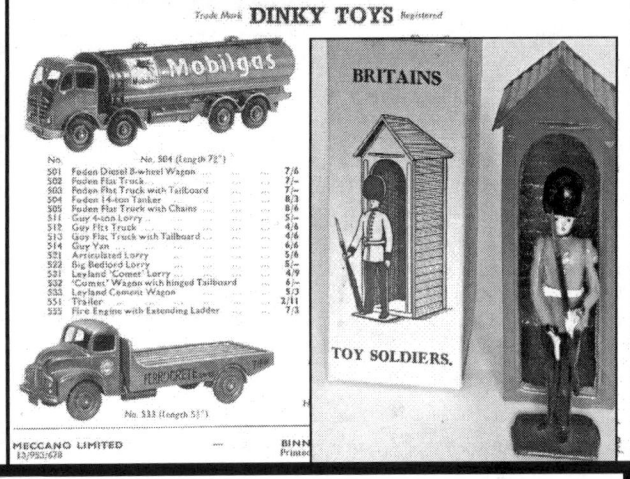

Britain is entitled to regard herself as the world's foremost toy factory. We export more toys than any other country and at home, out of every shilling now being spent in British toy shops only one penny is going into foreign manufacturers' pockets.

Judging from the splendid array of British toys now to be seen in provincial shops and in the big London stores, the toy trade was never in finer fettle. Manufacturers have been able to obtain the raw materials they want, and the result is a profusion of new and original toys, and improved versions of the old favourites, which ought to satisfy the most fastidious boy or girl. Since the war there have been complaints that the prices of toys had become too high. The public is also benefiting from the reduction in purchase tax from 33% to 25% brought in last year. This means that a toy which used to cost 10s 6d (53p) now costs 10s (50p) and there is a general tendency for prices to fall, thanks to the availability of materials.

Compared with war time Christmases, toys are either cheaper or better, or both. The best of them provide some answer to occasional criticisms of shoddy construction, and toys which have come here from abroad appear inferior by comparison. The emphasis placed this year on inter-planetary travel is too plain to be missed. It seems that almost any toy can be adapted to the space-travel theme, and even the malleable face of a puppet is recognisable as that of Mr Dan Dare, that most renowned of space travellers. Sets of "space men" in 7s 6d (38p) boxes are selling well, but this does not mean that any serious threat has arisen to the existence of toy soldiers who, of course, never die.

1954 Calendar

January
S	M	T	W	T	F	S
					1	2
3	4	5	6	7	8	9
10	11	12	13	14	15	16
17	18	19	20	21	22	23
24	25	26	27	28	29	30
31						

February
S	M	T	W	T	F	S
	1	2	3	4	5	6
7	8	9	10	11	12	13
14	15	16	17	18	19	20
21	22	23	24	25	26	27
28						

March
S	M	T	W	T	F	S
	1	2	3	4	5	6
7	8	9	10	11	12	13
14	15	16	17	18	19	20
21	22	23	24	25	26	27
28	29	30	31			

April
S	M	T	W	T	F	S
				1	2	3
4	5	6	7	8	9	10
11	12	13	14	15	16	17
18	19	20	21	22	23	24
25	26	27	28	29	30	

May
S	M	T	W	T	F	S
						1
2	3	4	5	6	7	8
9	10	11	12	13	14	15
16	17	18	19	20	21	22
23	24	25	26	27	28	29
30	31					

June
S	M	T	W	T	F	S
		1	2	3	4	5
6	7	8	9	10	11	12
13	14	15	16	17	18	19
20	21	22	23	24	25	26
27	28	29	30			

July
S	M	T	W	T	F	S
				1	2	3
4	5	6	7	8	9	10
11	12	13	14	15	16	17
18	19	20	21	22	23	24
25	26	27	28	29	30	31

August
S	M	T	W	T	F	S
1	2	3	4	5	6	7
8	9	10	11	12	13	14
15	16	17	18	19	20	21
22	23	24	25	26	27	28
29	30	31				

September
S	M	T	W	T	F	S
			1	2	3	4
5	6	7	8	9	10	11
12	13	14	15	16	17	18
19	20	21	22	23	24	25
26	27	28	29	30		

October
S	M	T	W	T	F	S
					1	2
3	4	5	6	7	8	9
10	11	12	13	14	15	16
17	18	19	20	21	22	23
24	25	26	27	28	29	30
31						

November
S	M	T	W	T	F	S
	1	2	3	4	5	6
7	8	9	10	11	12	13
14	15	16	17	18	19	20
21	22	23	24	25	26	27
28	29	30				

December
S	M	T	W	T	F	S
			1	2	3	4
5	6	7	8	9	10	11
12	13	14	15	16	17	18
19	20	21	22	23	24	25
26	27	28	29	30	31	

IF YOU ENJOYED THIS BOOK PLEASE LEAVE A RATING OR REVIEW AT AMAZON

Printed in Great Britain
by Amazon

e0a2c557-9f44-4681-b4c6-d28768e69ff9R01

Printed in Great Britain
by Amazon

NOTES